You
Watch
Too
Much
TV

You Watch Too Much TV

BUT DID YOU KNOW . . .

Ken Kessler

TAYLOR TRADE PUBLISHING

Lanham • New York • Dallas • Boulder • Toronto • Oxford

Published by Taylor Trade Publishing
An imprint of The Rowman & Littlefield Publishing Group, Inc.
4501 Forbes Boulevard, Suite 200
Lanham, Maryland 20706

Distributed by National Book Network

Library of Congress Cataloging-in-Publication Data

Kessler, Ken, 1965–
    You watch too much TV : but did you know— / Ken Kessler.—
1st Taylor Trade Publishing ed.
        p. cm.
    Includes bibliographical references and index.
    ISBN 1-58979-245-9 (pbk. : alk. paper)
    1. Television programs—United States—Miscellanea. I. Title.
PN1992.9.K47 2005
791.45'75'0973—dc22   2005002814

♾™ The paper used in this publication meets the minimum requirements
of American National Standard for Information Sciences—Permanence
of Paper for Printed Library Materials, ANSI/NISO Z39.48–1992.
Manufactured in the United States of America.

CONTENTS

INTRODUCTION

RADAR'S TEDDY BEAR

Do you have any idea what the name of Radar's teddy bear was? The odds are pretty good you don't know. I didn't. To be honest, I never gave it much thought. Then, the question came up on my morning radio show in Cincinnati. Before we took the first call, we admitted we didn't know the answer. We also emphatically stated that this was not a contest and there was no prize.

The phones exploded.

Each caller was certain that they knew the bear's name. They were 100 percent positive that they were right, because they watched M*A*S*H and they remembered the characters referring to the teddy bear by name.

Fuzzy. Pookie. Roosevelt.

We logged eighty-seven different names before we stopped writing them down. The calls kept coming around the clock. First, it was people certain they knew the bear's name. Then, they were calling to find out what the bear's name really was. This went on for days. Any contest or phone topic we tried to do was preempted by calls about that bear. A week later, we went to host a movie premiere, and people kept coming up to ask about Radar's bear. Then, we started getting calls from local TV stations and newspaper columnists. Everyone wanted to know the name of Radar's teddy bear.

Finally, I contacted Larry Gelbart. He developed M*A*S*H for television, along with writing and directing many episodes. He confirmed what we had begun to suspect. Radar's teddy bear did not have a name. We sighed with relief, figuring that it was finally over.

Two weeks later, a gentleman stopped by the station during the show. He told us that he had a friend who had a friend who had a friend, and he handed us a postcard. On the front was a scene from M*A*S*H, showing Radar hugging his teddy bear. On the back was the following message:

WARM 98 Gang,
My bear's name was Tiger.

Sincerely,
Gary Burghoff

I've worked at a bunch of radio stations, many of which have huge budgets for promotional events. I've given away trips, cars, and cash. I've sent people to see Celine Dion, Shania Twain, and the Rolling Stones. Not one of those events ever garnered the word of mouth that this one trivia question did.

A similar thing has been happening on TV recently. When the Reality TV trend hit a few years ago, celebrities were found hosting prime-time game shows that, for all their glamour and glitz, were little more than trivia contests. The questions that seemed to generate the most interest were the ones about TV shows. Regis asked about Full House (what city was the setting?). On The Weakest Link, Anne Robinson asked about Green Acres (what was the name of the Ziffel's pig?). I've even heard people argue over Phyllis and Rhoda (who left The Mary Tyler Moore Show first?).

Nielsen ratings consistently showed both Who Wants to Be a Millionaire and The Weakest Link as successes. Regis often placed two episodes in the top 5, while both programs routinely held four slots in the top 20. This was true even when they were reruns, by the way, proving there is a large interest in what these shows offer. And now, Regis returns during every sweeps period for special editions of his show, which is always a ratings' bonanza for ABC.

More recent ratings' winners are the current crop of reality programs. While *Survivor*'s appeal seems to be waning, *Queer Eye for the Straight Guy, American Idol,* and *The Apprentice* all seem to be generating the same kind of enthusiasm that grabbed audiences over twenty years ago, when everyone wanted to know who shot J. R.

Another new trend is the ever-increasing amount of television shows that are now appearing on DVD. There are the expected classics like *The Andy Griffith Show, M * A * S * H,* and *Cheers,* and fan-favorites like *The X-Files, Friends,* and *Buffy the Vampire Slayer.* There are also programs available from every age of television, including *I Love Lucy, The Monkees,* and *Charlie's Angels.* Current programs are even making their way onto DVD, like *Everybody Loves Raymond, Desperate Housewives,* and *Lost.*

It's not just that these shows are available; they're selling! Every week, more and more series become available. And more and more people welcome those shows they love back into their homes, where they can spend time with them again and again, whenever they want.

We all have strong feelings about TV shows. We may not remember who shot Mr. Burns or J. R. We may not know the name of Gilligan's boat or Frasier's son. We might not even remember on which soap Joey Tribiani appeared. But we think we do. Why? We watch too much TV. We don't just watch it; we become part of it. We care about these people and places that don't really exist. The programs take us away from our hectic, crazy lives. And we are so grateful.

Sometimes, it's only for thirty minutes, but a little break is better than none at all.

This escapism is evident even in the middle of summer, when reruns abound. On the threshold of political conventions, amid the ongoing war on terror and despite soaring gas prices, people tuned in night after night to cheer on Ken Jennings, the record-breaking champion on *Jeopardy.*

Every decade, TV trivia books hit the bookstores. Some focus on specific shows while others take a stab at a broader view. *You Watch Too Much TV* covers the total history of television in every section. It's *Jeopardy* for the rest of us!

Not only are you certain to find your favorites in every category, but you'll find many of them on every page! For example, the first chapter contains questions from the following programs: *Ally McBeal, M*A*S*H, Cheers, Just Shoot Me, The X-Files, Taxi, Quantum Leap, The Brady Bunch, Seinfeld,* and *ER*—and that's only the first three pages. That chapter alone covers three decades! *You Watch Too Much TV* runs the gamut from *The Honeymooners* to *Will and Grace*, from *You Bet Your Life* to *Last Comic Standing* and from *The Adventures of Ozzie and Harriet* to *The Osbournes*!

I have compiled one thousand questions, taken from years of radio contests, as well as from my own memory (I watch too much TV, too). The questions cover programs from television's infancy to the latest programs, including *Joey, CSI: New York,* and *Deadwood*.

The categories are as varied as the programs, including sections on spin-offs, kill-offs, sign-offs, aliens, lawyers, doctors, cops, dates, weddings, and babies. There are sections about shocking revelations, cliffhangers, and catch phrases. There's even a section about those "very special" episodes.

You Watch Too Much TV won't solve the world's problems. It won't make you smarter, thinner, or sexier. But, like the many programs it features, it can help you forget about your problems, if only for a little while.

Just in case you were wondering, *Full House* was set in San Francisco. The Ziffel's pig's name was Arnold. Rhoda left *The Mary Tyler Moore Show* first, in 1974 (Phyllis left one year later). Kristen shot J. R. Maggie shot Mr. Burns. Gilligan's boat was the SS *Minnow*. Frasier's son's name is Frederick. And Joey Tribiani appears on *Days of Our Lives*.

You probably already knew that. After all, You Watch Too Much TV.

PILOTS

The **pilot episode** is the first episode of a television show. In that first thirty or sixty minutes, they have to introduce the cast and the premise, and at the same time entertain enough so you'll come back next week. It's fun to look back at the way the long-running shows began. Some have gone through cast changes. Others have shifted the focus of the show. And some have changed the show completely.

How much do you remember about those first episodes?

1. Why did Ally quit her job and come to work for Cage and Fish on the first episode of *Ally McBeal*?
   a. She was being sexually discriminated against
   b. She was trying to get closer to Billy
   c. She was trying to get closer to John
   d. She was bored

2. Why were Hawkeye and Trapper trying to raise money on the first episode of *M*A*S*H*?
   a. To repair their still
   b. To send Radar to Seoul
   c. To send Ho Jon to college in the United States
   d. To pay off Henry's gambling debt

3. Where was Diane headed when she showed up on the pilot of *Cheers?*
   a. To the symphony
   b. To a foreign film festival
   c. To get married
   d. To a poetry reading

4. Who joined the staff of *Blush* magazine on the first episode of *Just Shoot Me?*
   a. Elliot
   b. Finch
   c. Nina
   d. Maya

5. Why was Scully partnered with Mulder in the pilot of *The X-Files?*
   a. She thought she was an abductee
   b. To kill him
   c. To discredit him
   d. To destroy any evidence he compiled

6. Whose first day on the job was part of the first episode of *Taxi?*
   a. Latka's
   b. Alex's
   c. Louie's
   d. John's

7. Who did Sam leap into on the first episode of *Quantum Leap?*
   a. Air Force pilot
   b. Blind piano player
   c. Lounge singer
   d. Hollywood stuntman

8. What was the name of the Brady girls' cat, who only appeared in the pilot of *The Brady Bunch*?
   a. Suzie
   b. Fluffy
   c. Tiger
   d. Snowball

9. What was the original name of *Seinfeld*, only used for the pilot?
   a. The Jerry Show
   b. The Seinfeld Chronicles
   c. Seinfeld Saga
   d. Seinfeld Stories

10. Who went on an interview to join a private practice on the first episode of *ER*?
    a. Doug
    b. Mark
    c. Benton
    d. Carter

11. What was the occasion for the party thrown for Murphy Brown on that show's first episode?
    a. Her return from having cosmetic surgery
    b. Her return from being in prison for protecting a source
    c. Her return from rehab
    d. Her return from being held hostage in the Middle East

12. What was the name of the roommate that moved out, allowing Jack to move in on the first episode of *Three's Company*?
    a. Janet
    b. Eleanor
    c. Helen
    d. Cindy

13. Where did Uncle Bill say he was going to send Buffy on the first episode of *Family Affair*?
   a. Back to Terra Haute
   b. To her aunt in Los Angeles
   c. To her grandparents in Chicago
   d. To boarding school in Switzerland

14. Who played the ship's doctor, Dr. O'Neill, on the first episode of *Love Boat*?
   a. Bernie Koppell
   b. Robert Reed
   c. Dick Van Patton
   d. Abe Vigoda

15. Why did Rachel need a place to live on the first episode of *Friends*?
   a. Lost her job
   b. Left her fiancé at the altar
   c. Lost her lease
   d. Left her husband when he announced he was gay

16. Who was the first to be voted off the island on the first episode of *Survivor*?
   a. Sonja Christopher
   b. Sean Kenniff
   c. B. B. Andersen
   d. Stacey Stillman

17. How long had Paul and Jamie been married on the first episode of *Mad About You*?
   a. Five weeks
   b. Five months
   c. Five years
   d. They weren't married, yet

18. What job was Mary Richards applying for on the pilot of *The Mary Tyler Moore Show?*
- **a.** Head writer
- **b.** Associate producer
- **c.** Executive producer
- **d.** Assistant news director

19. What was the first song WKRP played when they became a rock station in the first episode?
- **a.** "Locomotive Breath" by Jethro Tull
- **b.** "Kids Are Alright" by the Who
- **c.** "Queen of the Forest" by Ted Nugent
- **d.** "Lawyers, Guns and Money" by Warren Zevon

20. What job did Mimi apply for in the pilot of *The Drew Carey Show?*
- **a.** Assistant personnel director
- **b.** Perfume sprayer
- **c.** Lingerie department manager
- **d.** Cosmetician

ANSWERS			
1. a	**6.** d	**11.** c	**16.** a
2. c	**7.** a	**12.** b	**17.** b
3. c	**8.** b	**13.** d	**18.** b
4. d	**9.** b	**14.** c	**19.** c
5. c	**10.** b	**15.** b	**20.** d

"AND NO ONE CAN TALK TO A HORSE, OF COURSE"*

Pets have always been a big part of television. Sometimes, they were treated like a part of the family, as with the Flintstones's beloved Dino, Tony Baretta's cockatoo Fred, and Frasier's dad's terrier Eddie. Other times, the programs were built around the animals, like *Lassie*, *Mr. Ed*, and *Flipper*.

How much do you remember about these TV pets?

1. What female movie star did Dino fall in love with on *The Flintstones*?
   a. Rocka Welch
   b. Sassie
   c. Rock Beauty
   d. Belle

---

*from the theme song to *Mr. Ed*

2. On *7th Heaven*, where did the Camdens get Happy?
   a. The pound
   b. Annie's parents
   c. Moving neighbors
   d. Stray that followed Simon home

3. What was the name of the Munsters's pet dragon, which lived under the stairs?
   a. Rover
   b. Fido
   c. Spot
   d. George

4. What was Marcel's (Ross's monkey on Friends) favorite song?
   a. "Jungle Love"
   b. "The Lion Sleeps Tonight"
   c. "The Macarena"
   d. "Hakuna Matata"

5. On *The Andy Griffith Show*, what was the name of the bloodhound Barney used to track down an escaped criminal?
   a. Flash
   b. Fearless
   c. Blue
   d. Duke

6. Before Jamie and Paul moved in together, who owned Murray on *Mad About You*?
   a. Paul
   b. Jamie
   c. Ira
   d. Nat

7. Which of their seven dogs do *The Osbournes* consider "the gay one"?
   a. Minnie
   b. Lola
   c. Lulu
   d. Martini

8. Where did Sony's alligator, Elvis, come from on *Miami Vice*?
   a. Rescued from hotel pool
   b. Retired University of Florida mascot
   c. Wandered into police station
   d. Escaped from local tourist attraction

9. Where did Homer pick up Santa's Little Helper on *The Simpsons*?
   a. Parking lot outside a dog track
   b. Parking lot outside a mall
   c. Parking lot outside the fairgrounds
   d. Parking lot outside the power plant

10. Who was Porter Ricks?
    a. the father on *Lassie*
    b. the father on *Flipper*
    c. Rin Tin Tin's owner
    d. The man who sold Fred to *Baretta*

11. On *Malcolm in the Middle*, why did Craig pick Dewey to watch his cat Jellybean?
    a. Francis was away at military school
    b. Reese hated cats
    c. Malcolm was allergic to cats
    d. Jellybean liked Dewey the best

12. What pet did Arnold keep in his room on *Diff'rent Strokes*?
   a. Hamster named Abraham
   b. Tarantula named Abraham
   c. Goldfish named Abraham
   d. Guinea pig named Abraham

13. What kind of pet does Rory keep asking for on *8 Simple Rules for Dating My Teenage Daughter*?
   a. Dog
   b. Pony
   c. Monkey
   d. Cheetah

14. How did Kramer kill Phil's parrot Fredo on *Seinfeld*?
   a. Hid a key in his food dish, which Fredo ate
   b. Accidentally shot him with a crossbow
   c. Let Newman's cat out, who ate him
   d. Forgot to feed him while Phil was away

15. What was the real name of the dog that played Grendel, the Steadman's dog on *thirtysomething*?
   a. Maxx
   b. Mike
   c. Mack
   d. Murray

16. Who owned Arnold the pig on *Green Acres*?
   a. Fred and Doris Ziffel
   b. Sam Drucker
   c. Mr. Haney
   d. Eb Dawson

17. Who were Lassie's original owners in the early years of the series?
    a. the Martins
    b. the Millers
    c. Doc Weaver
    d. Cully Wilson

18. Why did Rudy want to leave her fish Lamont's funeral on *The Cosby Show*?
    a. She was too sad
    b. She wanted to go play with Bud
    c. She wanted to watch TV
    d. She wanted to eat lunch

19. What's the name of J. D. and Turk's stuffed dog on *Scrubs*?
    a. Rally
    b. Rowdy
    c. Raunchy
    d. Raleigh

20. Why did Kate want Drew's dog Speedy to go to obedience school on *The Drew Carey Show*?
    a. Couldn't be housebroken
    b. Wouldn't stay off the bed
    c. Didn't like her
    d. Didn't respond to his own name

ANSWERS			
1. b	6. a	11. d	16. a
2. a	7. d	12. c	17. b
3. c	8. b	13. c	18. c
4. b	9. a	14. a	19. b
5. c	10. b	15. a	20. c

"COME AND KNOCK ON OUR DOOR"*

Another important ingredient to storytelling is the wacky neighbor. This technique is almost exclusively used by sitcoms. Do you remember these strange but funny people next door?

1. What did Rob and Laura Petrie's neighbor, Jerry, do for a living on *The Dick Van Dyke Show*?
   a. Doctor
   b. Lawyer
   c. Dentist
   d. Mailman

2. On *Newhart*, what did Kirk say his only shortcoming was?
   a. Too good-looking
   b. Compulsive liar
   c. Lousy cook
   d. Too old for Leslie

---

*from the theme song to *Three's Company*

3. On the pilot for *Seinfeld*, what was Michael Richards's character's name?
   a. Cosmo
   b. Kelsey
   c. Kessler
   d. Crane

4. Where did Lenny and Squiggy work when *Laverne and Shirley* took place in Milwaukee?
   a. Frank's Pizza
   b. Shotz Brewery
   c. Cunningham Hardware
   d. Milwaukee Bowl

5. What kind of store did Ned Flanders open on *The Simpsons*?
   a. Religious bookstore
   b. Shop for left-handed people
   c. Shop for near-sighted people
   d. Starbucks

6. Who tried to get Mary to move so they could have her apartment on the pilot of *The Mary Tyler Moore Show*?
   a. Phyllis
   b. Sue Ann
   c. Ted
   d. Rhoda

7. Who did Gina say used to live in the apartment she got for Joey on *Joey*?
   a. Nicholas Cage
   b. Robert Deniro
   c. Tom Cruise
   d. Joe Pesci

8. What was the name of Jack's one-man show on *Will and Grace*?
   a. A Night with Jack
   b. Enough about Me, What Do You Think of Me?
   c. Just Jack
   d. Only Jack

9. On *Family Matters*, what was Urkell's first name?
   a. Sean
   b. Steve
   c. Bill
   d. Bob

10. On *Bewitched*, what was Gladys Kravitz's husband's name?
   a. Artie
   b. Arthur
   c. Abner
   d. Alan

11. What kind of housewarming present did Underhill give to Sam on *Cheers* when he took over the restaurant above the bar?
   a. Bottle of wine
   b. Doormat
   c. Gift certificate to the restaurant
   d. Card telling him never to come upstairs

12. On *Three's Company*, what was Mr. Furley's first name?
   a. Barney
   b. Warren
   c. Ralph
   d. Richie

13. Where in the city did Ralph Kramden's upstairs neighbor Ed Norton work on *The Honeymooners*?
   a. On telephone poles
   b. On a city bus
   c. In a city garbage truck
   d. In the city's sewers

14. How did Roger Healey discover the truth about Jeannie on *I Dream of Jeannie*?
   a. Dr. Bellows told him
   b. He rubbed her bottle while Tony was away and she popped out
   c. He overheard Tony talking to Jeannie about using her powers
   d. Jeannie's sister showed him

15. After playing Roger Healey on *I Dream of Jeannie*, Bill Dailey appeared as airline pilot Howard Borden on what show?
   a. *The Bob Newhart Show*
   b. *The Mary Tyler Moore Show*
   c. *The Jeffersons*
   d. *The San Pedro Beach Bums*

16. Why did Arthur keep sneaking into the house of the new neighbor (Lou Ferrigno) on *King of Queens*?
   a. To take pictures of him turning into the Hulk
   b. To get autographs to sell on eBay
   c. To try to get Lou to read his screenplay
   d. To take back the astronaut pen

17. Who suggested Kip and Henry move into the same hotel where she lived on *Bosom Buddies*?
   a. Sunny
   b. Isabel
   c. Lilly
   d. Amy

18. On *Mork and Mindy*, what did the downstairs neighbor, Mr. Bickley, do for a living?
    a. Television commercial writer
    b. Used car salesman
    c. Greeting card writer
    d. Insurance claims adjuster

19. Why do Frasier Crane and Cam Winston finally agree to stop feuding?
    a. Martin starts dating Cam's mother
    b. Eddie rescues Cam's Corgi
    c. Frasier convinces Cam to take an apartment in Niles's building
    d. Cam begins dating Maris

20. On *Sex and the City*, why did Samantha's neighbor Chip get arrested by the FBI?
    a. Committed credit card fraud (with her credit cards)
    b. Tax evasion
    c. Sent threatening e-mails to politicians on her computer
    d. Gave out inside stock info during sex

ANSWERS			
1. c	6. d	11. b	16. c
2. b	7. c	12. c	17. d
3. c	8. c	13. d	18. c
4. b	9. b	14. b	19. a
5. b	10. c	15. a	20. d

ENCIENTE

It seems difficult to believe now, but in television's early days, television couples didn't just sleep in separate beds, they couldn't even say the word "pregnant" on the air. In fact, censors were so cautious, the episode of *I Love Lucy* where Lucy went into labor was actually called *"Enciente,"* the Spanish word for pregnant. The word wasn't even permitted in the show's title (which audiences would never even see).

By contrast, on the first season of *Friends*, Ross splits from his wife because she's discovered she's a lesbian. A few episodes later, she announces that she's pregnant with Ross's child. The last episode of the season takes place in the hospital, with scenes in the delivery room, featuring Ross, his wife Carol, and her lesbian life-partner.

Light years from the days when even the word "pregnant" was considered risqué. How many of these TV pregnancies do you remember?

1. Who came up with the name "Mabel" for Paul and Jamie's baby on *Mad About You*?
   a. Paul's cousin Ira
   b. Jamie's mother
   c. Jamie's father
   d. Paul

2. Who played *Mork and Mindy*'s baby Mearth?
   a. Mel Brooks
   b. Carl Reiner
   c. Jonathan Winters
   d. Robin Williams

3. Why did Samantha have such a difficult time telling Darren that she was pregnant on *Bewitched*?
   a. Endora had turned him into a chicken
   b. Aunt Clara had turned him into a chimpanzee
   c. Dr. Bombay accidentally took her voice away
   d. Uncle Arthur transported him to Ancient Egypt

4. What song does Murphy Brown sing to her brand new baby in the hospital?
   a. "You Make Me Feel Like a Natural Woman"
   b. "One Fine Day"
   c. "The Way You Do the Things You Do"
   d. "Reach Out I'll Be There"

5. Where was Homer working when Marge told him she was pregnant with Maggie on *The Simpsons*?
   a. Nuclear power plant
   b. Moe's bar
   c. Miniature golf course
   d. Bowling alley

6. How does Gabe find out Julie's gone into labor on *Welcome Back, Kotter*?
   a. Julie's parents tell him
   b. Woodman announces it over the school's loudspeaker
   c. Barbarino interrupts his class to tell him
   d. Epstein presents it in a note from his mother

7. On *My Three Sons*, what branch of the service was Robbie in when Kate had the triplets?
   a. Army
   b. Navy
   c. Air Force
   d. Marines

8. Who was home with Lois when she went into labor with Jamie on *Malcolm in the Middle*?
   a. Francis
   b. Hal
   c. Malcolm
   d. Craig

9. On *Happy Days*, who does Lori Beth ask to be her birthing coach?
   a. Potsie
   b. Chachi
   c. Fonzie
   d. Roger

10. On *The Flintstones*, who did Wilma's mother send to help take care of baby Pebbles?
   a. Nurse Frightenshale
   b. Ann Margrock
   c. Lola Brickida
   d. Arnold the paper boy

11. Who suggests the name "Emily" for Kim and Greg's baby on *Yes, Dear*?
   a. Kim's mom
   b. Greg's dad
   c. Kim's dad
   d. Greg's mom

12. What happens to Sue Ellen's baby, John Ross, when she gets back from the hospital on *Dallas*?
    a. J. R. takes sole custody
    b. Pamela switches him with her baby
    c. Bobby takes him to work
    d. Cliff kidnaps him

13. On *Dharma and Greg*, what do Kitty and Edward give Abby and Larry for their new baby?
    a. Savings bond
    b. Nanny
    c. New van
    d. Complete silver service

14. What nickname does Shelly give her baby on *Northern Exposure*?
    a. Mandy-pandy
    b. The Pooper
    c. Little Holling
    d. Poopy

15. Who did Mary fear was Scott's real father on *Soap*?
    a. Alien Burt
    b. Chester
    c. Johnny
    d. Her English professor

16. Which of Alex's guests helped deliver Reed's baby on *Sisters*?
    a. Falconer
    b. Wynonna Judd
    c. Naomi Judd
    d. Faith Hill

17. As Fran goes into labor on *The Nanny*, what happens in her hospital room?
    a. Sheffield proposes
    b. Niles marries C. C.
    c. Sylvia and Yetta announce they're moving
    d. The kids leave for Europe

18. On *Sex and the City*, where was Carrie when Miranda went into labor?
    a. On a date with Big
    b. Spying on Richard with Samantha
    c. At a museum with Charlotte
    d. Buying shoes

19. What event is taking place as Maggie goes into labor on *Growing Pains*?
    a. Mike's first acting job
    b. Jason's award banquet
    c. Carol's graduation
    d. Ben's twelfth birthday party

20. Who takes Jenny to her last Lamaze class, where she goes into labor, on *The Jeffersons*?
    a. Tom
    b. George
    c. Lionel
    d. Florence

"DON'T DO THE CRIME IF YOU CAN'T DO THE TIME"*

Cop shows have long been a staple of prime-time television. In the earliest days, the programs focused more on the actual job of law enforcement. *Adam-12* and *Dragnet* took place solely on the beat. More recently, we've learned a lot more about the personal lives of those brave men and women behind the badge—whether it's a midday tryst with Frank and Joyce on *Hill Street Blues* or a shower scene with Andy Sipowicz on *NYPD Blue*. How much do you remember about these TV cops that promised to serve and protect?

1. Which precinct is home to *NYPD Blue*?
   a. 9th
   b. 12th
   c. 14th
   d. 15th

---

*from the theme song to *Baretta*

2. What was Tony Baretta's rank?
   a. Detective
   b. Lieutenant
   c. Sergeant
   d. Inspector

3. Where was *Ironside*, chief of detectives?
   a. Los Angeles
   b. New York
   c. San Francisco
   d. Chicago

4. How were Andy Taylor and Barney Fife related on *The Andy Griffith Show*?
   a. Cousins
   b. Brothers-in-law
   c. Stepbrothers
   d. They weren't related

5. Who got caught having sex in a squad car on *Third Watch*?
   a. Ty
   b. Bosco
   c. Faith
   d. Alex

6. What was Pepper's first name on *Police Woman*?
   a. Rita
   b. Suzanne
   c. Pepper
   d. Theresa

7. While *In the Heat of the Night* took place in Sparta, Mississippi, where did Virgil Tibbs get his big-city cop training?
   a. Boston
   b. Chicago
   c. Philadelphia
   d. Detroit

8. Who joined the cast following Michael Douglas's departure on the final season of *The Streets of San Francisco*?
   a. *Battlestar Galactica*'s Dirk Benedict
   b. *Battlestar Galactica*'s Richard Hatch
   c. *Miami Vice*'s Don Johnson
   d. *Miami Vice*'s Phillip Michael Thomas

9. Who played the role of Christine Cagney in the pilot of *Cagney and Lacey*?
   a. *Cheers'* Shelley Long
   b. *Baywatch*'s Pamela Anderson
   c. *Buck Rogers'* Erin Gray
   d. *M*A*S*H*'s Loretta Swit

10. On the first season of *Barney Miller*, who played the role of Janie Wentworth, the only female detective at the 12th Precinct?
    a. *Cagney and Lacey*'s Tyne Daley
    b. *Alice*'s Linda Lavin
    c. *Alice*'s Polly Holiday
    d. *Kate and Allie*'s Jane Curtain

11. How does Clay steal Will's badge on *Joan of Arcadia*?
    a. Lifts it while Joan works on the boat
    b. Takes it during Joan's yardsale
    c. Finds it when Will takes Kevin to a basketball game
    d. Sneaks it during Joan's chess match

12. What nickname did Starsky give Hutch's Ford Torino?
    a. Red Tornado
    b. Red Tomato
    c. Striped Tomato
    d. Striped Tornado

13. On *Everybody Loves Raymond*, how does Robert stop a hold-up at Nemo's while Ray is with him for a ride-along?
   a. Uses Ray as a decoy
   b. Throws hot pizza in the robber's face
   c. Hits the robber in the head with a beer pitcher
   d. Complains about his life until the robber gives up

14. Why did Ricardo Tubbs move from New York to Miami on *Miami Vice?*
   a. Chased the drug dealer that killed his brother
   b. Chased the hit man that killed his father
   c. Chased his ex-wife, who kidnapped his kids
   d. Chased the mob boss that killed his partner

15. What happened to Pete Malloy's partner, whom Jim Reed replaced, on *Adam-12?*
   a. He was killed on duty
   b. He was promoted
   c. He retired
   d. Malloy didn't have a partner before Reed

16. What was Kojak's first name?
   a. Frank
   b. Stephan
   c. Theo
   d. Cliff

17. Which two officers were actually assigned to Car 54 in *Car 54, Where Are You?*
   a. Toody and O'Hara
   b. O'Hara and Muldoon
   c. Schauser and Muldoon
   d. Toody and Muldoon

18. How did Mac's wife, Claire, die on *CSI: New York*?
    a. She was murdered by a serial killer from Miami
    b. She was killed in the World Trade Center on September 11th
    c. She was pushed in front of a subway train
    d. She disappeared five years ago, and no one knows what happened to her

19. On which one of the following programs did Richard Belzer's Detective Munch not appear?
    a. *Homicide: Life on the Street*
    b. *The X-Files*
    c. *Law and Order: Special Victims Unit*
    d. *NYPD Blue*

20. Why was T. J. Hooker assigned to train recruits?
    a. Disciplinary action after he wrecked a police car
    b. Disciplinary action after he shot the man that killed his partner
    c. Disciplinary action after he ticketed a senator
    d. Disciplinary action after he kills a suspect in a car accident

ANSWERS			
1. d	6. b	11. b	16. c
2. a	7. c	12. c	17. d
3. c	8. b	13. b	18. b
4. a	9. d	14. a	19. d
5. b	10. b	15. a	20. d

FROM BEDROCK TO SPRINGFIELD

In a lot of shows, the location is every bit as important as the characters. The program just wouldn't be the same in any other setting. Obviously, *Hogan's Heroes* had to take place in Germany, as *M*A*S*H* and *China Beach* needed to be set in Korea and Vietnam, respectively.

In others, the location simply becomes identifiable as the home of that series. What would a visit to Boston be without a stop at the *Cheers* bar? In Beverly Hills, while you may not see the Clampett's mansion, you'll still find yourself saying, "Swimming pools, movie stars." And in Minneapolis, you can even see a statue of Mary Richards.

How much do you remember about these real, and imagined, TV locations?

1. On *The Andy Griffith Show*, what real city did Barney Fife go to when he left Mayberry?
   a. Charlotte
   b. Raleigh
   c. Atlanta
   d. Houston

2. What state was the home to the Ingalls of Walnut Grove on *Little House on the Prairie*?
   a. Minnesota
   b. Kansas
   c. Wisconsin
   d. Nebraska

3. What was the name of the high school the Sweathogs attended on *Welcome Back, Kotter*?
   a. Woodrow Wilson High
   b. James McKinley High
   c. James Madison High
   d. James Buchanan High

4. On what street in Queens did the Bunkers live in *All in the Family*?
   a. Hargett
   b. Hauser
   c. Huntley
   d. Huntington

5. Who lived at 1313 Mockingbird Lane?
   a. The Munsters
   b. The Addams Family
   c. The Flintstones
   d. The Simpsons

6. What city was the setting for *Dark Shadows*?
   a. Collinwood, Maine
   b. Collinsport, Maine
   c. Crab Apple Cove, Maine
   d. Cabot Cove, Maine

7. Which show was not set in Ohio?
   a. *Family Ties*
   b. *Drew Carey Show*
   c. *One Day at a Time*
   d. *3rd Rock from the Sun*

8. Which POW camp was Col. Klink in command of on *Hogan's Heroes*?
   a. Stalag 13
   b. Stalag 15
   c. Stalag 17
   d. Stalag 19

9. What was the name of the high school featured on *Room 222*?
   a. Robert Frost High School
   b. Walt Whitman High School
   c. Henry David Thoreau High School
   d. Washington Irving High School

10. Which San Francisco hotel was home to Paladin on *Have Gun, Will Travel*?
    a. Hotel Carlton
    b. St. Gregory Hotel
    c. Shady Rest Hotel
    d. Blackstone Hotel

11. While Metropolis and Gotham City were both based on New York City, what superhero actually lived and fought crime in the Big Apple?
    a. Incredible Hulk
    b. Wonder Woman
    c. Spider-man
    d. The Flash

12. What was the name of the ranch that was home to the Ewings on *Dallas*?
    a. Southland
    b. Southfork
    c. Southampton
    d. South Hills

13. Which building does WKRP broadcast from (in Cincinnati)?
    a. Flynn Building
    b. Flimm Building
    c. Carlson Building
    d. Wren Building

14. Who lives at 742 Evergreen Terrace in the mythical city of Springfield?
    a. Homer Simpson
    b. Ned Flanders
    c. Montgomery Burns
    d. Moe Szyslak

15. What was the name of the L.A. bookstore that Ellen managed on *Ellen*?
    a. Ellen's Books
    b. These Books of Mine
    c. Buy the Book
    d. Book 'Em

16. Which series took place in Boston?
    a. *Perry Mason*
    b. *Rockford Files*
    c. *The Practice*
    d. *CSI: Crime Scene Investigation*

17. Which series did *not* take place in Boston?
    a. *Taxi*
    b. *Cheers*
    c. *Ally McBeal*
    d. *The Practice*

18. What's the name of the shoe store where Al works in *Married . . . with Children?*
    a. Larry's Shoes and Accessories for the Beautiful Woman
    b. Harry's Shoes and Accessories for the Beautiful Woman
    c. Garry's Shoes and Accessories for the Beautiful Woman
    d. Barry's Shoes and Accessories for the Beautiful Woman

19. What store acted as the secret entrance for *The Man From U.N.C.L.E.?*
    a. Del Florist Shop
    b. Del Floria Tailor Shop
    c. Del Flores Antiques
    d. Del Floren Travel Agency

20. Who lived at 1334 North Beechwood Drive in Los Angeles?
    a. Jed Clampett
    b. Arnie Becker
    c. Buffy Summers
    d. The Monkees

ANSWERS			
1. b	6. b	11. c	16. c
2. a	7. c	12. b	17. a
3. d	8. a	13. b	18. c
4. b	9. b	14. a	19. b
5. a	10. a	15. c	20. d

"WHEN YOU CONTROL THE MAIL, YOU CONTROL INFORMATION"*

Part of what makes it so easy to identify with so many TV characters is that they, like us, have jobs. For some, the job is simply one more facet of their personality. Ray Barone was a sports writer on *Everybody Loves Raymond*; Mike Brady was an architect on the *Brady Bunch*; Jim Anderson was an insurance salesman on *Father Knows Best*. These jobs were rarely part of the shows.

On the other hand, the majority of episodes of some shows occurred entirely at the workplace. Almost every episode of *Cheers* took place at Sam's bar. Barney Miller episodes were confined to the squad room for almost the entire run of the series. And Columbo was so wrapped up in his job, that he was never even given a first name (other than Lieutenant)!

---

*Newman from *Seinfeld*

How much do you remember about these characters and their jobs?

1. How long had Kramer been on strike from H&H Bagels on *Seinfeld*?
    a. 10 years
    b. 11 years
    c. 12 years
    d. 13 years

2. On *Two Guys, a Girl, and a Pizza Place*, what was the name of the pizza place?
    a. Pizza Place
    b. Beacon Street Pizza
    c. Fifth Street Pizza
    d. Dunville Pizza

3. For which department of Winfred-Lauder did Drew work on *The Drew Carey Show*?
    a. Bookkeeping
    b. Cosmetics
    c. Accounting
    d. Personnel

4. What job did Oliver Douglas leave when he bought the farm on *Green Acres*?
    a. Doctor
    b. Lawyer
    c. Accountant
    d. Advertising Executive

5. What was Tony Nelson's rank at the beginning of *I Dream of Jeannie*?
    a. Lieutenant
    b. Captain
    c. Major
    d. Colonel

6. What did Bob's friend Jerry do for a living on *The Bob Newhart Show*?
   a. Dentist
   b. Optometrist
   c. Gynecologist
   d. Proctologist

7. What was Benson's original job when he joined the governor's staff?
   a. In charge of the kitchen staff
   b. In charge of the grounds keeping staff
   c. In charge of the household staff
   d. In charge of the governor's children

8. On *Designing Women*, what kind of business was Sugarbakers?
   a. Interior Design
   b. Landscaping Design
   c. Graphic Design
   d. Kitchen Design

9. What was the name of the ad agency on *Melrose Place*?
   a. Woodward Advertising
   b. Stedman Advertising
   c. D&D Advertising
   d. McMahon and Tate Advertising

10. On *Coach*, what job did Hayden Fox take that had him move away from Minnesota State?
    a. Head coach of the Miami Dolphins
    b. Head coach of the Miami Hurricanes
    c. Head coach of the Orlando Marlins
    d. Head coach of the Orlando Breakers

11. Who was George Jetson's boss on *The Jetsons*?
    a. Mr. Spacely
    b. Mr. Sprockets
    c. Mr. Slate
    d. Mr. Burns

12. What was the name of the delivery company that Doug works for on *King of Queens*?
    a. UPS
    b. IPS
    c. Speedy Delivery
    d. Federal Express

13. What agency, pretending to be part of the CIA, first recruited Sydney on *Alias*?
    a. SD-6
    b. SD-9
    c. SD-12
    d. SD-13

14. On the *The Brady Bunch*, what did Mike Brady do to solve a family problem that nearly cost him a million dollar deal with Mr. Crawford?
    a. Forbid the kids from using the phone
    b. Replaced the home phone with a pay phone
    c. Let Greg use his car while Marcia took the station wagon
    d. Took the entire family away on a camping trip

15. What was the name of the ad agency Michael and Elliot worked for on *thirtysomething*?
    a. Drentel and Ashley
    b. Drentel and Stedman
    c. Drentel, Arthur, and Ashley
    d. Miles Drentel and Associates

16. What was the name of Fred's business on *Sanford and Son*?
    a. Sanford Salvage
    b. Sanford and Son Salvage
    c. Sanford and Son Antiques
    d. Elizabeth's Antiques and Collectibles

17. What company does Hank Hill work for on *King of the Hill*?
    a. Arlen Propane
    b. Texas Propane
    c. American Propane
    d. Strickland Propane

18. Who ran Colby Enterprises on *The Colbys*?
    a. Blake Carrington
    b. Jason Colby
    c. Zach Powers
    d. Jeff Colby

19. Before the car crash put him into a coma, what did Johnny Smith do for a living on *The Dead Zone*?
    a. Science teacher
    b. Social studies teacher
    c. English teacher
    d. Chemistry teacher

20. What did Wilbur Post do for a living on *Mister Ed*?
    a. Writer
    b. Insurance salesman
    c. Architect
    d. Accountant

ANSWERS			
1. c	6. a	11. a	16. b
2. b	7. c	12. b	17. d
3. d	8. a	13. a	18. b
4. b	9. c	14. b	19. a
5. b	10. d	15. c	20. c

SAME BAT TIME, SAME BAT CHANNEL

To be continued.... Three words that flash across the screen, usually at the moment that the hero is in the worst peril—Fonzie's motorcycle flying into the air over the trash cans, the Brady boys getting caught by Vincent Price in Hawaii, or a shadowy figure pulling the trigger on J. R.

How much do you remember about these cliff-hangers?

1. On *Dallas*, who shot J. R.?
   a. Bobby Ewing
   b. Jock Ewing
   c. Cliff Barnes
   d. Kristin Shepard

2. While Jessica was found guilty, who actually killed Peter Campbell on *Soap*?
   a. Chester Tate
   b. Danny Dallas
   c. Burt Campbell
   d. Jodie Dallas

3. Even though everyone in Springfield had a motive, who actually shot Mr. Burns on *The Simpsons*?
   a. Waylon Smithers
   b. Moe Szyslak
   c. Sideshow Bob
   d. Maggie Simpson

4. Who set off a bomb in the apartment complex on *Melrose Place*?
   a. Brooke Armstrong
   b. Kimberly Shaw
   c. Jo Beth Reynolds
   d. Richard Hart

5. Which members of the *Jupiter 2* crew did the Keeper want to add to his collection on *Lost in Space*?
   a. Don and Judy
   b. Penny and Will
   c. Judy and Penny
   d. Dr. Smith and Will

6. Who pushed Karen off the back of her boat on *Will and Grace*?
   a. Jack
   b. Rosario
   c. Lorraine
   d. Danni

7. Who takes custody of Evil Dick, escorting him off the planet, on *3rd Rock from the Sun*?
   a. Don Orville
   b. Dennis Rodman
   c. Liam Neesam
   d. Stone Phillips

8. Who revived Steve Austin after he passed out on the trail of Bigfoot on *The Six Million Dollar Man*?
   a. Oscar Goldman
   b. Jaimie Sommers
   c. Bigfoot's alien creators
   d. Rudy Wells

9. How many garbage cans does Fonzie fly his motorcycle over on *Happy Days*?
   a. 11
   b. 12
   c. 13
   d. 14

10. What message does Jack get too late as he and Salazar flee in the helicopter on *24*?
    a. Palmer is safe
    b. Kyle Singer is in custody
    c. Chase is freed
    d. The virus was recovered

11. Who, played by Phil Silvers, offers to sell Central Park to Jed on *The Beverly Hillbillies*?
    a. Honest John
    b. Holloway
    c. Matthew Templeton
    d. Shorty

12. Who helps Cindy and Bobby when they get lost in the Grand Canyon on *The Brady Bunch*?
    a. Zacchariah T. Brown
    b. Sam the butcher
    c. Jimmy
    d. Mike

13. On *M*A*S*H*, who was Hawkeye trying to say goodbye to when B. J. Honeycutt arrived?
  a. Henry Blake
  b. Trapper John McEntyre
  c. Radar O'Reilly
  d. Frank Burns

14. When Zoey is kidnapped and President Bartlett steps down, who assumes the power of the Presidency on *The West Wing*?
  a. Glenallan Walken
  b. John Hoynes
  c. Leo McGarry
  d. Toby Ziegler

15. What two super villains teamed up on *Batman*, trying to dispatch the caped-crusaders by first crushing him with a giant meteorite and then feeding him to a giant clam?
  a. Joker and Catwoman
  b. Penguin and Catwoman
  c. Catwoman and Riddler
  d. Penguin and Joker

16. Who played Paul Hollister, an art thief, that *Charlie's Angels* track on a Caribbean cruise, featuring cast members of the *Love Boat*?
  a. Bert Convy
  b. Abe Vigoda
  c. Dick Sargent
  d. Tom Bosley

17. On *Knots Landing*, who found Val after Jill made her overdose of sleeping pills?
  a. Gary Ewing
  b. Michael Fairgate
  c. Frank Williams
  d. Brian Cunningham

18. At a battle at Wolf 359, who saves Picard by putting the
    Borg to sleep on *Star Trek: The Next Generation?*
    a. Sisko
    b. Riker
    c. Data
    d. Troi

19. Although Buffy was arrested for the murder of Kendra, who
    actually killed her on *Buffy the Vampire Slayer?*
    a. Spike
    b. Drusilla
    c. Angel
    d. Acathla

20. Who unties George and Weezy after a burglar ties them up
    on *The Jeffersons?*
    a. Florence
    b. Mr. Bentley
    c. Helen Willis
    d. Edith Bunker

ANSWERS			
1. d	**6.** c	**11.** a	**16.** a
2. a	**7.** b	**12.** c	**17.** c
3. d	**8.** c	**13.** b	**18.** c
4. b	**9.** d	**14.** a	**19.** b
5. b	**10.** b	**15.** d	**20.** a

"WE'RE MOVIN' ON UP"*

Just as sequels are big business for the movie business, spin-offs are huge for television. Many programs that find success try to mine that popularity by giving new shows to popular characters. Frasier Crane made the jump from *Cheers*, as Benson did from *Soap* and Gomer Pyle did from *The Andy Griffith Show*.

If that's not possible, they still try to launch a series that is somehow tied to the successful series, even if it's a one-time appearance by a character—Mork was only on a single episode of *Happy Days*, Sheriff Andy Taylor was on one episode of *Make Room for Daddy*, and Horatio Caine appeared once on *CSI: Crime Scene Investigation*.

How many of these did you even remember were spin-offs?

1. Why did Laverne and Shirley first appear on *Happy Days*?
   a. Dates for Fonzie and Richie
   b. Contestants in a beauty contest at Arnold's
   c. Ralph and Potsie meet them while touring a brewery
   d. They enter a dance contest at Arnold's

---

*from the theme song to *The Jeffersons*

2. On another *Happy Days* spin-off, Mork tells Mindy about meeting Fonzie, who set him up on a date with whom?
   a. Joanie Cunningham
   b. Jenny Piccolo
   c. Laverne DeFazio
   d. Shirley Feeney

3. Before he got his own show, what did Frasier Crane tell everyone at *Cheers* about his father?
   a. He was a cop
   b. He was a lawyer
   c. He was a writer
   d. He was dead

4. On the *Friends'* spin-off *Joey,* what TV show did Joey Tribiani turn down when he moved to L.A.?
   a. *Mac and C.H.E.E.S.E.*
   b. *Bloody Cop*
   c. *Chimp and the Baseball Player*
   d. *Nurses*

5. Whose execution-style murder led cast members from *CSI: Crime Scene Investigation* to Florida, introducing Horatio Caine and launching the spin-off *CSI: Miami*?
   a. Duke Rittle
   b. Frank McBride
   c. Bob Martin
   d. Larry Maddox

6. Before they had their own show, *The Simpsons* appeared as shorts on what program?
   a. *In Living Color*
   b. *Tracy Ullman Show*
   c. *Mad TV*
   d. *Arsenio*

7. When Denise left *The Cosby Show* and went to *A Different World*, what college was she attending?
   a. Hillman College
   b. Mumford College
   c. Loyola College
   d. New York University

8. Where was Trapper John the chief of surgery, once he left *M*A*S*H* and got his own show?
   a. Chicago Memorial
   b. San Francisco Memorial
   c. San Diego Memorial
   d. Houston Memorial

9. In what state does Russell Greene run into Tess from *Touched by an Angel*, sending him and his family on their mission that became the series *Promised Land*?
   a. Kentucky
   b. Colorado
   c. Wyoming
   d. Arkansas

10. Why did Florida Evans tell Maude she was leaving, launching her series *Good Times*, a spin-off of *Maude*, which was a spin-off of *All in the Family*?
    a. She was pregnant
    b. Her husband got a promotion
    c. She was moving to Chicago to take care of her mother
    d. She was going to work in a restaurant

11. Which *All in the Family* cast member was the last to say good-bye to the Jeffersons?
    a. Archie
    b. Edith
    c. Gloria
    d. Mike

12. On what show did Hondo and his Special Weapons and Tactics Unit first appear, before they got their own show, *S.W.A.T.*?
   a. *Police Woman*
   b. *Emergency*
   c. *The Rookies*
   d. *Adam-12*

13. Why does Sheriff Andy Taylor arrest Danny Thomas on *Make Room for Daddy*?
   a. Speeding
   b. Failing to signal
   c. Running a stop sign
   d. Running a red light

14. When Gomer Pyle joined the Marines, Sheriff Andy Taylor tagged along and led Sgt. Carter to believe Gomer was related to whom?
   a. President Johnson
   b. General Lucis Pyle
   c. General Douglas MacArthur
   d. J. Edgar Hoover

15. What school did Mrs. Garrett go to as headmistress when she left the Drummonds on *Diff'rent Strokes*?
   a. Jefferson
   b. Lincoln
   c. Northern
   d. Eastland

16. How did Jessica Tate (*Soap*) get Governor Gene Gatling to give Benson a job?
   a. She contributes money to his campaign
   b. They're cousins
   c. He's in love with her
   d. They were high school sweethearts

17. Before Kevin James was on *King of Queens* he appeared on *Everybody Loves Raymond*, as well as which one of these other programs?
   a. *Cosby*
   b. *Cybill*
   c. *Step by Step*
   d. *The Nanny*

18. Who was the only character to travel from *Beverly Hills 90210* to *Melrose Place*?
   a. Jake Hanson
   b. Billy Campbell
   c. Jane Andrews
   d. Alison Parker

19. Who fired Alan Shore on *The Practice*, setting up the launch of the spin-off *Boston Legal*?
   a. Ellenor Frutt
   b. Bobby Donnell
   c. Eugene Young
   d. Helen Gamble

20. Why did Rhoda leave Minneapolis (and the *The Mary Tyler Moore Show*) and decide to stay in New York?
   a. She got a job offer
   b. She met Joe
   c. She missed her sister
   d. Her mother made her feel guilty about moving away

ANSWERS			
1. a	**6.** b	**11.** b	**16.** b
2. c	**7.** a	**12.** c	**17.** a
3. d	**8.** b	**13.** c	**18.** a
4. d	**9.** a	**14.** b	**19.** c
5. a	**10.** b	**15.** d	**20.** b

THE DOCTOR WILL SEE YOU NOW

Medical programs have been around since the golden days of radio, and they easily made the jump to the small screen—from the comedies like *Doc Corkle* to the dramas like *City Hospital* to the slew of soaps that centered around the goings-on of hospitals and their medical staffs. Some fifty years later, it's still a popular subject—from the comedies like *Scrubs*, to the dramas like *Nip/Tuck* to the soaps that still populate the daytime airwaves.

How much do you remember about these shows about those in the medical profession?

1. What is the name of the hospital on *ER*?
   a. Chicago General Hospital
   b. Cook County General Hospital
   c. County General Hospital
   d. Daley General Hospital

2. Where did *M*A*S*H*'s Hawkeye Pierce do his medical residency?
   a. Boston
   b. Bangor
   c. Chicago
   d. New York

3. What test does Doogie pass on the first episode of *Doogie Howser, MD*?
   a. College Boards
   b. Med Final
   c. SAT
   d. Driver's License

4. What kind of doctor was Cliff Huxtable on *The Cosby Show*?
   a. Obstetrician
   b. Pediatrician
   c. Optometrist
   d. Dentist

5. Who was Marcus Welby in love with during the first season of *Marcus Welby, MD*?
   a. Myra Sherwood
   b. Kathleen Faverty
   c. Sandy Porter
   d. Janet Blake

6. How did *St. Elsewhere* conclude its run?
   a. The hospital was taken over by Ecumena Hospitals Corporation
   b. The hospital was condemned and torn down
   c. The hospital was destroyed when a helicopter crashed into the top floor
   d. The entire series turned out to be a figment of Tommy Westphall's imagination

7. Who was chief of staff on *Chicago Hope*?
   a. Dr. Watters
   b. Dr. Geiger
   c. Dr. Shutt
   d. Dr. Austin

8. Where did *Northern Exposure*'s Joel Fleishman go to medical school?
   a. NYU
   b. Harvard
   c. Princeton
   d. Columbia

9. Why was Ben Casey's love interest, Jane Hickcock, at County General Hospital?
   a. She was a nurse
   b. She was a patient who had awakened from a thirteen-year coma
   c. She was a patient recovering from surgery
   d. She was the niece of Dr. Zorba

10. How did Dr. Kildaire become a patient at Blair General?
    a. His appendix became inflamed and nearly burst
    b. He caught a virus and had to be quarantined
    c. He tripped over a cart looking at a nurse's aide
    d. He was in a car accident, hit by a drunk driver

11. On *Trapper John, MD*, who else besides Trapper served in a M*A*S*H unit?
    a. Gonzo Gates
    b. Jacob Christmas
    c. Stanley Riverside II
    d. Jackpot Jackson

12. Who became chief of staff of Wilshire Memorial as *Melrose Place* ended it's run?
    a. Peter Burns
    b. Michael Mancini
    c. Irene Shulman
    d. Dan Hathaway

13. Who played medical student Alex Smith on *Diagnosis Murder*?
    a. Barry Van Dyke, Dick Van Dyke's son
    b. Barry Van Dyke, Dick Van Dyke's grandson
    c. Shane Van Dyke, Dick Van Dyke's son
    d. Shane Van Dyke, Dick Van Dyke's grandson

14. On the first episode of *Nip/Tuck*, what did McNamera say is wrong with the butt implant that Troy was performing?
    a. Patient's body rejected it
    b. Insurance forms were filled out wrong
    c. It was performed on the wrong patient
    d. It was put in upside down

15. What was *Becker*'s first name?
    a. Sam
    b. Jack
    c. John
    d. Steve

16. On *Scrubs*, who operates on J. D. when he's admitted with appendicitis?
    a. Turk
    b. Cox
    c. Kelso
    d. Todd

17. What event led Dr. Quinn to head west to the Colorado territory?
    a. Gold rush
    b. Death of her father
    c. Death of her husband
    d. Her friend, Charlotte, was gravely ill

18. On *Emergency!*, what hospital provided backup for Squad 51?
    a. L.A. County General
    b. L.A. Memorial
    c. Ramdale Hospital
    d. Rampart Hospital

19. At the end of *Empty Nest*'s run, why was Harry Weston headed to Vermont?
    a. To open a new clinic with Laverne
    b. To work at a children's hospital
    c. To accept a teaching job
    d. To get away from Charley once and for all

20. Who gets Jordan the job offer to come back to Boston on *Crossing Jordan*?
    a. Garret Macy
    b. Bug
    c. Nigel Townsend
    d. Trey Sanders

ANSWERS			
1. c	**6.** d	**11.** a	**16.** a
2. a	**7.** a	**12.** b	**17.** b
3. d	**8.** d	**13.** d	**18.** d
4. a	**9.** b	**14.** d	**19.** c
5. a	**10.** c	**15.** c	**20.** a

"I'M LIVING ON THE AIR IN CINCINNATI"*

Another staple of television has been its obsession with its own medium. Behind-the-scenes shows have focused on newspapers, magazines and, probably the most popular, shows within shows.

How much do you remember about these shows about the media?

1. What award was Les Nessman the most proud on *WKRP in Cincinnati*?
   a. Golden Pig Award
   b. Silver Sow Award
   c. Blue Ribbon Chuck Wagon Award
   d. Buckeye Newsman Award

---

*from the theme song to *WKRP in Cincinnati*

2. When Lou Grant got fired from WJM/Minneapolis, what L.A. newspaper did he go to?
   a. *L.A. Times*
   b. *L.A. News*
   c. *L.A. Post*
   d. *L.A. Tribune*

3. What's wrong with the sports anchor Mary hired on *The Mary Tyler Moore Show?*
   a. She mispronounced too many names
   b. She bashed Minneapolis and its citizens
   c. She thought sports were stupid
   d. She only covered swimming events

4. What led to Jim Dial quitting FYI on *Murphy Brown?*
   a. Network censorship on his tobacco exposé
   b. Stan refusing his request for a raise
   c. Solidarity with the firing of Miles
   d. Job offer from a rival news program

5. Which newspaper landed on Gary's doorstep on *Early Edition?*
   a. *Sun-Times*
   b. *Tribune*
   c. *Daily News*
   d. *Post*

6. Why was everyone at KACL fired on *Frasier?*
   a. Frasier was negotiating contracts
   b. Format flip to "Salsa"
   c. New owners automated the station
   d. FCC fined for indecent programming

7. Who did Kolchak write for on *Kolchak: The Night Stalker*?
   a. Chicago's Independent News Service
   b. Chicago's United News Service
   c. Chicago's Associated News Service
   d. Chicago's Independent Press Service

8. In what publication does Carrie Bradshaw's "Sex and the City" column appear?
   a. *New York Post*
   b. *New York Daily News*
   c. *New York Magazine*
   d. *New York Star*

9. On *Lois and Clark: The New Adventures of Superman*, who was the only one of the following that, at one time or another, did not own *The Daily Planet*?
   a. Lex Luther
   b. Franklin Stern
   c. Leslie Luckabee
   d. Perry White

10. What was Tim O'Hara's job on *My Favorite Martian*?
    a. Reporter for L.A. radio station KABC
    b. Reporter for L.A. newspaper *The Sun*
    c. Reporter for L.A. television station KABC
    d. Reporter for L.A. magazine *Review*

11. Who was a late-night radio personality on CERK?
    a. Johnny Fever before he went to *WKRP in Cincinnati*
    b. Murphy Brown before she went to FYI
    c. Lucien LaCroix, Nick's nemesis on *Forever Night*
    d. Jack Killian after he quit the police force on *Midnight Caller*

12. What magazine did Don Hollinger, Ann Marie's boyfriend, work for on *That Girl*?
   a. *Newsview*
   b. *Newsday*
   c. *News and Views*
   d. *Newsweek*

13. Who was the music critic for San Francisco's *The Gate* magazine on *Suddenly Susan*?
   a. Susan Keane
   b. Jack Richmond
   c. Luis Rivera
   d. Todd Stites

14. On what network did *Sports Night*, the show within the show, air?
   a. Continental Sports Channel
   b. United Sports Network
   c. Global Sports Channel
   d. ESPN

15. What's the name of Tony Kleinman's show within the show on *Listen Up*?
   a. Shut Up and Listen
   b. Listen Up
   c. Listening to Sports
   d. Sport Look and Listen

16. On *The Dick Van Dyke Show*, who was the head writer of *The Alan Brady Show*?
   a. Buddy Sorrell
   b. Sally Rogers
   c. Rob Petrie
   d. Mel Cooley

17. What was the name of the Sacramento publication that Tom Bradford's column appeared in on *Eight Is Enough*?
   a. *Sacramento Weekly*
   b. *The Register*
   c. *The Picayune*
   d. *Sacramento Times*

18. Who was the owner of radio station WNYX on *Newsradio*?
   a. Jimmy James
   b. Bill McNeal
   c. Dave Nelson
   d. Joe Garelli

19. Who did Ira hire to narrate Paul's documentary *Buchman* on *Mad About You*?
   a. Robin Williams
   b. Billy Crystal
   c. Tom Hanks
   d. James Earl Jones

20. What city was home to radio station WENN on *Remember WENN*?
   a. Boston
   b. Philadelphia
   c. Pittsburgh
   d. Cleveland

ANSWERS			
1. b	**6.** b	**11.** c	**16.** c
2. d	**7.** a	**12.** a	**17.** b
3. d	**8.** d	**13.** d	**18.** a
4. a	**9.** d	**14.** a	**19.** d
5. a	**10.** b	**15.** b	**20.** c

"They're Creepy and They're Kooky"*

amilies are another staple of television. From the Nelsons to the Osbournes, the Ricardos to the Simpsons and the Cleavers to the Sopranos, we've seen countless versions of TV families. It didn't matter where, or if, either or both parents worked. It didn't matter how good the kids were in school or sports. It only mattered that they had each other. Most of the time. Even on *Married . . . with Children*.

How much do you remember about these TV families?

1. How was Fester related to Gomez and Morticia on *The Addams Family*?
   a. Morticia's brother
   b. Morticia's uncle
   c. Gomez's uncle
   d. Gomez's brother

---

*from the theme song to *The Addams Family*

2. How was Marilyn related to Herman and Lily on *The Munsters*?
   a. Lily's niece
   b. Herman's niece
   c. Lily's stepdaughter
   d. Herman and Lily's daughter

3. Who was Nicky and Alex's father on *Full House*?
   a. Danny
   b. Jesse
   c. Joey
   d. Nick

4. On *American Dreams*, who was the child whose father, Jack Pryor, forbid from appearing on *American Bandstand*?
   a. Roxanne
   b. Beth
   c. Patty
   d. Meg

5. Which of the Huxtable children found a lost dog and tried to convince Cliff to let them keep it on *The Cosby Show*?
   a. Theo
   b. Vanessa
   c. Rudy
   d. Olivia

6. Which of Fonzie's relatives gave him a robe from the Orient one Christmas on *Happy Days*?
   a. His mother
   b. His father
   c. Chachi
   d. Spike

7. Which of the Brady kids was picked to be a safety monitor on *The Brady Bunch*?
   a. Peter
   b. Jan
   c. Bobby
   d. Cindy

8. Who played Shirley Partridge's father, occasionally seen on *The Partridge Family*?
   a. Ray Bolger
   b. Bert Lahr
   c. Jack Haley
   d. Dave Madden

9. On *Father Knows Best*, whose teacher quit their job to follow a dream of writing?
   a. Betty's
   b. Bud's
   c. Kathy's
   d. Jim's

10. Which of the Douglas children was the first to get married on *My Three Sons*?
    a. Mike
    b. Chip
    c. Robbie
    d. Ernie

11. How are Jimmy and Christine related to Greg and Kim on *Yes, Dear*?
    a. Jimmy and Greg are brothers
    b. Christine and Kim are sisters
    c. Greg and Christine are siblings
    d. Jimmy and Kim are siblings

12. Which member of the Miller family was diagnosed with depression on *Still Standing*?
    a. Brian
    b. Lauren
    c. Linda
    d. Judy

13. Which member of the Cleaver family played the clarinet on *Leave It to Beaver*?
    a. Ward
    b. June
    c. Wally
    d. Beaver

14. Which member of the Bundy family got glasses after they drove into a lake on *Married . . . with Children*?
    a. Al
    b. Peg
    c. Kelly
    d. Bud

15. Who was the only member of the Jetson family that didn't want a dog on *The Jetsons*?
    a. George
    b. Jane
    c. Judy
    d. Elroy

16. What leads Jill to talk to Tim about having another baby on *Home Improvement*?
    a. Mark refused to bake cookies with her
    b. Randy wanted to go on his first date
    c. Brad got his driver's license
    d. Her sister Carol is about to have a baby girl

17. Which of the Bradley ladies married Steve the crop duster on *Petticoat Junction?*
  a. Kate
  b. Bobbie Jo
  c. Billie Jo
  d. Betty Jo

18. Why did Tony's son A. J. get suspended from school on *The Sopranos?*
  a. He was caught selling drugs
  b. He was caught cheating on a test
  c. He was caught drinking sacramental wine
  d. He was caught making out with a girl in a confessional

19. On *Roseanne,* while Dan takes Becky clothes shopping, how does Roseanne try to bond with Darlene?
  a. They watch a boxing match together
  b. They watch a basketball game together
  c. They watch an animation festival together
  d. They watch a horror movie double feature together

20. Who played Alex Keaton's Uncle Ned, who was wanted by the FBI for embezzlement, on *Family Ties?*
  a. Michael Keaton
  b. Billy Crystal
  c. Tom Hanks
  d. Peter Scolari

ANSWERS			
1. b	**6.** b	**11.** b	**16.** d
2. a	**7.** c	**12.** b	**17.** d
3. b	**8.** a	**13.** d	**18.** c
4. d	**9.** d	**14.** a	**19.** b
5. c	**10.** a	**15.** a	**20.** c

SPACE:
THE FINAL FRONTIER

Television had a fascination with space long before
Captain Kirk. *Buck Rogers* and *Flash Gordon* made the jump
to TV early on. Ralph Kramden dressed as a man from
space on an episode of *The Honeymooners*, and Lucy and Ethel pretended to be women from Mars on *I Love Lucy*.

Since then, we watched real men walk on the moon. We got
used to aliens living among us, including Mork, Alf, and the
Solomon family on *3rd Rock from the Sun*. And now in the twenty-first century, we have multiple *Stargates*, a remake (and updated)
Battlestar Galactica and the fifth series from the *Star Trek* universe.

How much do you know about these TV shows set in and
around space?

1. While Ralph dressed as a man from space on *The Honeymooners*,
   what did his lodge think he was trying to be?
   a. Knight
   b. Washing machine
   c. Pinball machine
   d. Army tank

2. What was Mork's mission on *Mork and Mindy?*
   a. To find Exidor
   b. To study earth women
   c. To study emotions
   d. To study Earthlings

3. According to *Stargate Atlantis*, where was the legendary island of Atlantis?
   a. Antarctica
   b. Africa
   c. Australia
   d. Japan

4. Which *Star Trek* spin-off changed the opening words from "Where no man has gone before" to "Where no *one* has gone before"?
   a. *Deep Space Nine*
   b. *The Next Generation*
   c. *Voyager*
   d. *Enterprise*

5. Who was the human traitor that collaborated with the Cylons on *Battlestar Galactica?*
   a. Tigh
   b. Baltar
   c. Dr. Zee
   d. Cain

6. What did the "V" stand for on the 1980s series *V?*
   a. Vanquished
   b. Villagers
   c. Visitors
   d. Vanished

7. Which of the aliens was the Intelligence Specialist on *3rd Rock from the Sun*?
   a. Dick
   b. Sally
   c. Harry
   d. Tommy

8. On the final episode of *The X-Files*, when did the Cigarette Smoking Man say that the aliens would invade and take over the Earth?
   a. 2010
   b. 2011
   c. 2012
   d. 2013

9. According to *Buck Rogers in the 25th Century*, when did Buck originally leave Earth?
   a. 1987
   b. 1999
   c. 2001
   d. 2010

10. On *Stargate SG-1*, where is Earth's only Stargate?
    a. Roswell, New Mexico
    b. Cheyenne, Wyoming
    c. Area 51
    d. Fort Knox, Kentucky

11. What was the *Jupiter II*'s original destination on *Lost in Space*?
    a. Pluto
    b. Star Base VII
    c. Alpha Centauri
    d. Planet X

12. Who was the only member of Martin's family to appear on *My Favorite Martian*?
   a. Nephew Andy
   b. Cousin Andy
   c. Little brother Andy
   d. Stepson Andy

13. What planet did *Deep Space Nine* orbit on the *Star Trek* spin-off?
   a. Cardassia
   b. Bajor
   c. Ferengi
   d. Tyree

14. On *Space: 1999*, what sent the moon hurtling through space away from Earth?
   a. Nuclear explosion
   b. Rogue planet Meta
   c. Unmanned spacecraft *Voyager*
   d. Brian the computer

15. What was Alf's real name?
   a. Alfonse
   b. Alfa Shumway
   c. Gordon Shumway
   d. Gordon Sumner

16. What space craft did Captain Tony Nelson eject from that led to his finding Jeannie on *I Dream of Jeannie*?
   a. *Mercury 9*
   b. *Stardust I*
   c. *Aries 7*
   d. *Moon Rocket I*

17. On *Farscape*, what was the name of John Crichton's ship, which took him through a wormhole to the world of the Peacekeepers?
    a. *Aries 7*
    b. *Stardust I*
    c. *Moya*
    d. *Farscape*

18. According to *Star Trek: Enterprise*, when did the Vulcans first have contact with humans?
    a. 1947
    b. 1957
    c. 1967
    d. 1977

19. Who appeared on the final episode of *Galactica 1980* in an attempt to save the series?
    a. Starbuck
    b. Adama
    c. Apollo
    d. Baltar

20. Where was *Voyager* when it was transported into the uncharted Delta Quadrant on *Star Trek: Voyager*?
    a. Neutral Zone
    b. Forbidden Zone
    c. Badlands
    d. Alpha Quadrant

ANSWERS

1. c	6. c	11. c	16. b
2. d	7. d	12. a	17. d
3. a	8. c	13. b	18. b
4. b	9. a	14. a	19. a
5. b	10. b	15. c	20. c

DATING GAMES

In the early days of television, dating was something that was almost exclusively for the kids. Slowly, it turned out that the first-date angst we all felt as teens could be pretty funny if transferred to adults. This concept continued until entire shows were built around that quest for the perfect relationship.

How many of these TV dating do's and don't's do you remember?

1. Who was Ross dating on *Friends* when Rachel first realized how he had felt about her?
   a. Julie
   b. Bonnie
   c. Emily
   d. Charlie

2. On *Happy Days*, where did Richie meet Lori Beth?
   a. Arnold's
   b. Cunningham Hardware
   c. Library
   d. Prom

3. Who was the first girl Brandon dated after the Walsh family moved to *Beverly Hills 90210*?
   a. Kelly
   b. Jackie
   c. Andrea
   d. Marianne

4. Who was the last woman *Frasier* dated as that series ended?
   a. Charlotte
   b. Nanny G
   c. Ann
   d. Lilith

5. What happened the day after Lauren dumped Alex on *Family Ties*?
   a. He graduated high school
   b. He graduated college
   c. He met Marty
   d. He went on a date with Marty

6. How was Bud learning to dance for his date with Marcia on *Father Knows Best*?
   a. His dad was teaching him
   b. His mom was teaching him
   c. Betty was teaching him
   d. He was learning from a book

7. Who was the first woman Eddie fixed his dad up with on *The Courtship of Eddie's Father*?
   a. Miss Allen
   b. Lynn Bardman
   c. Dolly Daly
   d. Mrs. Livingston

8. Which one of the Brady kids worried that getting braces was the reason for a broken date on *The Brady Bunch*?
   a. Greg
   b. Marcia
   c. Peter
   d. Jan

9. On *Boy Meets World*, for what event did Corey spend all night waiting in line for tickets?
   a. Limp Bizkit concert
   b. World Series
   c. Da Vinci retrospective
   d. Van Gogh retrospective

10. What did Ben write in Felicity's high school yearbook after "I would have said keep in touch, but unfortunately . . . "?
    a. I'm moving to New York
    b. I don't know who you are
    c. We were never in touch
    d. I'm in love with someone else

11. Who did Dawson invite as his date to the "prom" he, Joey, and Andie threw on *Dawson's Creek*?
    a. Joey
    b. Jen
    c. Andie
    d. Gail

12. On *Spin City*, who dumped Caitlin, leading her to kiss Charlie for the first time?
    a. Mike
    b. Tim
    c. Rob
    d. Jason

13. Who did Charlie try to date in an effort to keep Jake from getting suspended from school on *Two and a Half Men?*
    a. His pediatrician
    b. His principal
    c. His tutor
    d. His teacher

14. On the last episode of *Sex and the City*, what was Bigg's real name revealed to be?
    a. Jim
    b. John
    c. Jack
    d. Jeff

15. What happened to *Cybill's* Oscar night date, after he left her at the ceremony?
    a. He got arrested soliciting a prostitute
    b. He got arrested buying drugs
    c. He went out with Maryann
    d. He made a pass at Maryann

16. Which talk show host played Laverne's boyfriend Joey on *Laverne and Shirley?*
    a. David Letterman
    b. Jay Leno
    c. Bill Mahr
    d. Phil Donahue

17. Who was the first person Ryan dated on *The OC?*
    a. Marissa
    b. Julie
    c. Theresa
    d. Hailey

18. Why did Marla (The Virgin) dump Jerry on *Seinfeld*?
   a. He accused her of having breast implants
   b. He refused to wear her "puffy shirt" on *The Tonight Show*
   c. She made him choose between the fake voice and her
   d. She found out about The Contest

19. Who did Barney Fife pretend to be dating in an attempt to make Thelma Lou jealous on *The Andy Griffith Show*?
   a. Helen
   b. Ellie
   c. Juanita
   d. Gloria

20. Who invited Diane to go to Paris with him, leading her and Sam to get together for the first time on *Cheers*?
   a. Frasier Crane
   b. Sam's brother Derek
   c. Sam's cousin Derek
   d. Sumner Sloan

ANSWERS			
1. a	**6.** d	**11.** a	**16.** b
2. c	**7.** c	**12.** b	**17.** a
3. d	**8.** b	**13.** d	**18.** d
4. a	**9.** d	**14.** b	**19.** c
5. b	**10.** c	**15.** a	**20.** b

I DO

There aren't many more pivotal events than weddings, and television has been full of them, season after season. The situation is full of opportunities for conflict, perfect for drama and comedy. You wonder who might speak up when asked during the ceremony "if there's anyone with any reason. . . ." And you identify with the couple as they plow through the minutiae in planning such an event.

How much do you remember about these TV weddings?

1. Who forgot to pick up *Rhoda* for her wedding?
   a. Mary
   b. Georgette
   c. Phyllis
   d. Brenda

2. In the final episode of *Mad About You*, when Paul and Jamie found out they weren't legally married, what guest star performed the official (and legal) ceremony?
   a. Lyle Lovett
   b. Mel Brooks
   c. Sid Caesar
   d. Tim Conway

3. Who interrupted Mike and Carol's wedding on the first episode of *The Brady Bunch*?
   a. Tiger and Fluffy
   b. Carol's parents
   c. Greg, Peter, and Bobby
   d. Marcia, Jan, and Cindy

4. Who wasn't present at Ross and Emily's wedding on *Friends*?
   a. Phoebe
   b. Joey
   c. Rachel
   d. Chandler

5. Where did Grace and Leo first exchange vows on *Will and Grace*?
   a. Plaza Hotel
   b. Central Park
   c. Catskills
   d. Hospital

6. Who did Niles and Daphne run into at the courthouse before their civil ceremony on *Frasier*?
   a. Donny, Daphne's ex-fiancé
   b. Meg, Niles's ex-fiancée
   c. Maris
   d. Daphne's parents

7. Who got married in Vegas after breaking up Chris and Jane's wedding on *Melrose Place*?
   a. Billy and Alison
   b. Michael and Jane
   c. Michael and Kimberly
   d. Billy and Brooke

8. What happened to the tape of Ray and Debra's wedding on *Everybody Loves Raymond*?
   a. Ray taped the Super Bowl over it
   b. Ray taped the World Series over it
   c. Ray taped the Stanley Cup over it
   d. Ray taped the Olympics over it

9. What holiday was approaching as Syd and Owen got married on *Providence*?
   a. Valentine's Day
   b. Easter
   c. July 4th
   d. Christmas

10. Why didn't Jeannie want pictures of her wedding to Tony on *I Dream of Jeannie*?
    a. Genies don't photograph
    b. Her sister was jealous
    c. Her former master was jealous
    d. Her sister was the photographer

11. Who got married at the end of the *Baywatch* reunion movie, *Baywatch Hawaiian Wedding*?
    a. Mitch and Neely
    b. Mitch and Allison
    c. Mitch and C. J.
    d. C. J. and Lorenzo

12. Who left *Charlie's Angels* to get married, paving the way for Shelley Hack to join the team?
    a. Jill Munroe
    b. Sabrina Duncan
    c. Kelly Garret
    d. Tiffany Welles

13. On *Taxi*, who cured Latka of his multiple personality disorder so he and Simka could get married?
- **a.** Jim Ignatowski
- **b.** Bob Newhart (as Dr. Hartley)
- **c.** Dr. Joyce Brothers
- **d.** Alex Reiger

14. Who set Christine's wedding dress on fire on *Coach*?
- **a.** Luther
- **b.** Hayden
- **c.** Dauber
- **d.** Howard

15. Who did Carla take to her ex-husband Nick's wedding on *Cheers*?
- **a.** Woody
- **b.** Sam
- **c.** Frasier
- **d.** Eddie

16. Who got married on the first episode of *Dynasty*?
- **a.** Cecil and Alexis
- **b.** Jeff and Fallon
- **c.** Blake and Krystal
- **d.** Prince Michael and Amanda

17. Why did Daisy agree to marry Enos on *The Dukes of Hazzard*?
- **a.** So she wouldn't have to testify against him
- **b.** So Enos wouldn't move away
- **c.** So Boss Hogg would finally leave the Dukes alone
- **d.** So the Dukes wouldn't lose their farm after Jesse passed away

18. Who was Best Man at Mike and Sully's wedding on *Dr. Quinn Medicine Woman*?
- **a.** Brian
- **b.** Cloud Dancing
- **c.** Custer
- **d.** Robert E

19. Who nearly kept Max from making it to his own wedding on *Get Smart*?
- **a.** Dr. Madre, an escaped KAOS agent
- **b.** Admiral Hargrade
- **c.** The Chief
- **d.** The Chameleon, KAOS master of disguise

20. Who interrupted Lois's wedding to Lex Luther on *Lois and Clark: The New Adventures of Superman*?
- **a.** Clark Kent
- **b.** Jimmy Olsen
- **c.** Perry White
- **d.** Inspector Henderson

ANSWERS			
1. c	**6.** a	**11.** d	**16.** c
2. d	**7.** c	**12.** b	**17.** a
3. a	**8.** a	**13.** c	**18.** b
4. a	**9.** d	**14.** a	**19.** a
5. b	**10.** a	**15.** b	**20.** c

"SIT ON IT"

Many TV shows find ways to work their way into the mainstream lexicon. Popular characters develop catch phrases that catch on, sometimes by accident. Sometimes, the phrases become more popular than the shows. "Cowabunga, dude!" started showing up on T-shirts long before *The Simpsons* garnered any ratings success. Occasionally, the phrases even outlive the programs from which they came.

How many of these TV catch phrases can you match with the programs from which they came?

1. "Not that there's anything wrong with that."
2. "Nanoo, Nanoo."
3. "You're fired."
4. "Fuhgetaboutit."
5. "Sit on it."
6. "Is that your final answer?"
7. "Up your nose with a rubber hose."
8. "Did I do that?"
9. "Nip it in the bud."
10. "Sha-zamm!"
11. "Some day, I'm gonna have to have a long talk with that boy."
12. "I don't think so, Tim."
13. "Dy-no-mite!"

14. "You can take that to the bank."
15. "Who loves ya, baby?"
16. "You are the weakest link. Goodbye."
17. "How you doin'?"
18. "Whatchu talkin' about, Willis?"
19. "Book him, Dan-O."
20. "They killed Kenny! Those bastards!"

a. *Andy Griffith Show*
b. *Baretta*
c. *Friends*
d. *The Apprentice*
e. *Diff'rent Strokes*
f. *South Park*
g. *Sopranos*
h. *Happy Days*
i. *Mork and Mindy*
j. *Gomer Pyle*
k. *Home Improvement*
l. *Seinfeld*
m. *Who Wants to Be a Millionaire?*
n. *Good Times*
o. *Welcome Back, Kotter*
p. *Beverly Hillbillies*
q. *Kojak*
r. *The Weakest Link*
s. *Hawaii Five-O*
t. *Family Matters*

ANSWERS			
1. l	6. m	11. p	16. r
2. i	7. o	12. k	17. c
3. d	8. t	13. n	18. e
4. g	9. a	14. b	19. s
5. h	10. j	15. q	20. f

POISONED INVITATIONS AND ELEVATOR SHAFTS

Sometimes a character just has to go. There can be many reasons. The actor could want out of their contract. The show could want the actor out of their contract. Or the character might just have gone as far as they could go.

Then again, it could be as simple as a ratings stunt. Or, in a sick way, it could just be very funny.

How much do you remember about these shows and the characters they killed off?

1. On *M*A*S*H*, which one of these characters was killed on their way home from the war?
   a. Major Frank Burns
   b. Captain Trapper John MacIntyre
   c. Lt. Col. Henry Blake
   d. Corporal Walter "Radar" O'Reilly

2. Marring the celebration of Nancy's cancer surgery, who was killed in an accident on *thirtysomething*?
  a. Gary
  b. Michael
  c. Elliott
  d. Billy

3. How did Chuckles the Clown die on *The Mary Tyler Moore Show*?
  a. Drowned by a selzter bottle
  b. Poisoned by bad pies
  c. Crushed by an elephant
  d. Suicide after his show was cancelled

4. An apparent victim of Maggie's curse, how does Rick die on *Northern Exposure*?
  a. Hit by a falling satellite
  b. Froze to death on a glacier
  c. Poisoned by picnic potato salad
  d. Struck by lightning on oil rig

5. Where did Paul Hennessey die on *8 Simple Rules*, after actor John Ritter died?
  a. Newspaper office
  b. Grocery store
  c. Highway
  d. Football stadium

6. On *Friends*, why did *Days of Our Lives* kill off the character Joey was playing?
  a. His egotistical interview in *Soap Opera Digest*
  b. He was demanding too much money
  c. He was demanding too many perks, including sandwiches in his dressing room
  d. He slept with one of the writers, then dumped her

7. How did Carla's husband Eddie get killed off on *Cheers*?
   a. Run over by the Zamboni
   b. Poisoned by his other wife
   c. Fell out of plane doing promotional stunt
   d. Licked envelope with toxic glue

8. Who did George call after Susan died on *Seinfeld*?
   a. Her parents
   b. Jerry
   c. His parents
   d. Marisa Tomei

9. What was the name of the *L.A. Law* episode where Rosalind fell down the elevator shaft?
   a. "The Fall of Rosalind Shays"
   b. "Dropping Out"
   c. "Good to the Last Drop"
   d. "Those You Meet on the Way Down"

10. What object struck Maude Flanders, sending her to her death on *The Simpsons*?
    a. T-shirt fired from T-shirt cannon
    b. Piece of car from crash during race
    c. Beer can thrown to, and missed by, Homer
    d. Falling piece of satellite

11. What did Bobby Simone die of on *NYPD Blue*?
    a. Shot by alcoholic Detective Walsh
    b. Cancer
    c. Stabbed by rape suspect
    d. Complications from heart surgery

12. On *Ally McBeal*, where did Billy Thomas die?
    a. His office
    b. The bar
    c. In court
    d. At Ally's apartment

13. Even though it turned out to be a dream, who killed Bobby Ewing on *Dallas*?
   a. Katherine Wentworth
   b. Donna Culver
   c. Jamie Ewing
   d. Sue Ellen Ewing

14. How did James Evans die on *Good Times*?
   a. Car accident
   b. Cancer
   c. Heart attack
   d. Stroke

15. Although her death didn't happen on the show, how did Edith Bunker die on *Archie Bunker's Place*?
   a. Heart attack
   b. Stroke
   c. Cancer
   d. Car accident

16. In what kind of store was Speed killed on *CSI: Miami*?
   a. Pawn shop
   b. Gun shop
   c. Jewelry store
   d. Drug store

17. When Prudence died on *Charmed*, who joined the Halliwell sisters, restoring the Power of Three?
   a. Piper
   b. Paige
   c. Phoebe
   d. Patty

18. On *ER*, who was killed by a helicopter?
    a. Lucy Knight
    b. Doug's dad, Ray Ross
    c. Dr. Romano
    d. Dr. Gant

19. How was Sgt. Phil Esterhaus written out of the show after the actor passed away on *Hill Street Blues*?
    a. Shot during a robbery attempt
    b. Stabbed during robbery attempt
    c. Shot by jealous husband
    d. Heart attack during sex

20. How did Mrs. Landingham die on *The West Wing*?
    a. Cancer
    b. Stroke
    c. Heart attack
    d. Car accident

ANSWERS			
1. c	6. a	11. d	16. c
2. a	7. a	12. c	17. b
3. c	8. d	13. a	18. c
4. a	9. c	14. a	19. d
5. b	10. a	15. b	20. d

THINGS THAT GO "BUMP" ON TV

Just because you're dead, doesn't mean you have to stay dead. At least, on TV. Ghosts, witches, and vampires have been all over television. Sometimes, they're played seriously. Sometimes for laughs. And sometimes, it's supposed to be serious, but we can't help laughing, anyway.

How much do you remember about these ghostly shows?

1. Ed Asner and Lily Tomlin guest-starred on the *X-Files* as ghosts trying to kill Scully and Mulder on what holiday?
   a. Halloween
   b. Christmas
   c. St. Valentine's Day
   d. Easter

2. At her senior prom, what award did Buffy receive on *Buffy the Vampire Slayer*?
   a. Most Likely to Succeed
   b. Most Admired
   c. Class Protector
   d. Community Protector

3. Who originally made *Angel* a vampire?
   a. Doyle
   b. Darla
   c. Justine
   d. Spike

4. What was the name of Sydney Hansen's mother, whose ghost appeared to her throughout the series on *Providence*?
   a. Lisa
   b. Lauren
   c. Lynda
   d. Laura

5. When Endora first meets Darrin on *Bewitched*, what does she threaten to turn him into?
   a. Artichoke
   b. Pumpkin
   c. Celery stalk
   d. Head of cabbage

6. On the last season of *The Munsters*, which wedding anniversary did Lily and Herman celebrate?
   a. 10th
   b. 25th
   c. 50th
   d. 100th

7. On the last season of *The Addams Family*, which wedding anniversary do Morticia and Gomez celebrate?
   a. 12th
   b. 13th
   c. 14th
   d. 15th

8. Who releases Barnabas Collins from his coffin on *Dark Shadows*?
   a. Willie Loomis
   b. Victoria Winters
   c. Dr. Julia Hoffman
   d. Angelique DuBois

9. On the first episode of the original *Outer Limits*, what job did Cliff Robertson's character have that helped him in contacting aliens?
   a. Scientist
   b. Astronaut
   c. Radio station engineer
   d. Television station engineer

10. Who starred in *Night Gallery*'s spin on "The Phantom of the Opera"?
    a. Burgess Meredith
    b. Leslie Neilsen
    c. Lloyd Bridges
    d. Arte Johnson

11. What character did Bill Mumy revisit, in a sequel to his original episode, on the 2002 version of the *Twilight Zone*?
    a. Ron Howard
    b. Anthony Fremont
    c. William Shatner
    d. Arte Johnson

12. Who was head of the Witch's Council during the first season of *Sabrina the Teenaged Witch*?
    a. Hilda
    b. Zelda
    c. Irma
    d. Drell

13. On *Twin Peaks*, who did Killer Bob not murder?
  a. Laura Palmer
  b. Theresa Banks
  c. Maddy Ferguson
  d. Annie Blackburn

14. What singer did Billy's ghost tell Ally to go on a date with on *Ally McBeal*?
  a. Sting
  b. Barry White
  c. Barry Manilow
  d. Josh Groban

15. Who originally played the vampire detective Nicholas Night on the pilot of *Forever Night*?
  a. David Hasselhoff
  b. Rick Springfield
  c. Shaun Cassidy
  d. David Cassidy

16. What was Carl Kolchak's greatest fear on *Kolchak: The Night Stalker*?
  a. Heights
  b. Snakes
  c. Dentists
  d. Ghosts

17. On *Charmed*, who was Chris named after?
  a. Leo's dad
  b. Wyatt's dad
  c. Jason's dad
  d. Darryl's dad

18. On the first "Treehouse of Horror" on *The Simpsons*, who voiced the narration for Lisa's reading of "The Raven"?
    a. Tony Bennett
    b. James Earl Jones
    c. Kelsey Grammar
    d. Phil Hartman

19. On *The Ghost and Mrs. Muir*, what was the name of the ghost?
    a. Captain Horatio Figg
    b. Captain Daniel Gregg
    c. Captain Claymore Gregg
    d. Captain Deke Tuttle

20. How did Johnny's mother die on *The Dead Zone*?
    a. Suicide
    b. Reverend Purdy killed her
    c. Stillson killed her
    d. She died in a car accident

ANSWERS			
1. b	**6.** d	**11.** b	**16.** c
2. c	**7.** b	**12.** d	**17.** a
3. b	**8.** a	**13.** d	**18.** b
4. c	**9.** c	**14.** d	**19.** b
5. a	**10.** b	**15.** d	**20.** a

LONDON, BABY!

Many shows, usually sitcoms, take the cast to new locations. Sometimes it's a ratings stunt; sometimes it's an attempt to revive a struggling series. Much has been made about Fonzie "jumping the shark" on *Happy Days*. What's usually left out is that the cast was on a trip to California, taking the show away from Milwaukee—a rarity for the series. *The Brady Bunch* went to the Grand Canyon and Hawaii in memorable three-part episodes. *Friends* took a two-part trip to London. And Lucy and Ricky, Fred and Ethel all went to Hollywood for almost twenty episodes!

How much do you remember about these shows that went on location?

1. What English celebrity did Joey run into when *Friends* went to London for Ross's wedding to Emily?
   a. Prince William
   b. Prince Harry
   c. Sarah Ferguson
   d. Elton John

2. Why did the Keatons travel to London on *Family Ties*?
   a. Alex got a study scholarship at Oxford
   b. Steven had an interview with the BBC
   c. Mallory wanted to attend a fashion expo
   d. Ellyse was asked to speak at an international architecture conference

3. Which of the Bradys found the bad luck idol in Hawaii on the *Brady Bunch*?
   a. Bobby
   b. Peter
   c. Greg
   d. Mike

4. Why did *The Facts of Life* crew head to Paris?
   a. Blair had run away to find her father
   b. Mrs. Garrett wanted to attend a cooking school
   c. Jo won the trip in a radio contest
   d. Natalie got a writing scholarship

5. When *The Partridge Family* went to King's Island amusement park in Cincinnati, which Partridge got sick on all the rides?
   a. Shirley
   b. Keith
   c. Reuben
   d. Danny

6. Who treated the whole family to a trip to Italy on *Everybody Loves Raymond*?
   a. Marie
   b. Frank
   c. Ray
   d. Robert

7. When he winds up trapped in China, what was Drew relieved to find on *The Drew Carey Show*?
   a. Pay phone
   b. American embassy
   c. Beer
   d. McDonalds

8. When the *Happy Days* gang headed to Hollywood, who did the studio want to sign?
   a. Richie
   b. Fonzie
   c. Potsie
   d. Joanie

9. What was the name of the movie Ricky Ricardo was supposed to star in, which led the cast to California on *I Love Lucy*?
   a. *Singing Cowboy*
   b. *Singing Detective*
   c. *Don Juan*
   d. *Kissing Bandit*

10. Whose wedding got called off, as the cast went to Las Vegas on *Designing Women*?
    a. Mary Jo
    b. Julia
    c. Suzanne
    d. Anthony

11. When the Seavers went to Europe, who was hospitalized with appendicitis on *Growing Pains*?
    a. Jason
    b. Maggie
    c. Mike
    d. Carol

12. While in Hawaii, why did George decide he should sell his business on *The Jeffersons*?
    a. His doctor told him to lower his blood pressure
    b. Japanese businessman made him a deal
    c. Louise asked him to sell
    d. He hated New York and wanted to move

13. Why did the Bundys win a trip to England on *Married . . . with Children*?
    a. Al won Shoe Salesman of the Year
    b. Villagers want to kill Al and Bud to stop a curse
    c. Kelly's rich old boyfriend left them the money in his will
    d. Peg won it on a TV game show

14. Why did the Kyles nearly miss their flight home from Hawaii on *My Wife and Kids*?
    a. Michael got the flight times wrong
    b. Jr. wanted to stay with his new girlfriend
    c. Kady couldn't find her doll, Little Pippy
    d. All of the above

15. Whose grandfather owned a hotel in Hawaii, where everyone stayed on *Saved by the Bell*?
    a. Zack
    b. Screech
    c. Kelly
    d. Jessie

16. Why did Jed want to buy Central Park on *The Beverly Hillbillies*?
    a. To find a new suitor for Ellie May after her wedding was called off
    b. It reminded the family of home
    c. Granny thought the New York squirrels made the best vittles
    d. Jethro decided he wanted to be a star on Broadway

17. Why do Jim and Cheryl go on a Disney Cruise on *According to Jim*?
    a. Gracie won a contest on the Disney Channel
    b. Dana cast them in a TV commercial
    c. Jim surprised Cheryl with the trip, since she'd always wanted to go
    d. Cheryl surprised Jim with the trip, since he'd always wanted to go

18. When *The Love Boat* went to Alaska, which crew member became obsessed with Alaska trivia?
    a. Gopher
    b. Doc
    c. Isaac
    d. Capt. Stubing

19. Why was Richard in a hospital in Spain on *Caroline in the City*?
    a. Trampled during the running of the bulls
    b. Gored by a bull in a bullfight
    c. Appendicitis
    d. Food poisoning

20. What record did Flash set at Disney World on *Step by Step*?
    a. Most rides ridden in a single weekend
    b. Most hot dogs eaten in Tomorrowland
    c. Most continuous rides on Space Mountain
    d. Most ice cream eaten in one day

ANSWERS			
1. c	**6.** a	**11.** b	**16.** a
2. a	**7.** d	**12.** a	**17.** b
3. a	**8.** a	**13.** b	**18.** c
4. b	**9.** c	**14.** d	**19.** a
5. b	**10.** d	**15.** c	**20.** a

"IS THAT YOUR FINAL ANSWER?"*

Game shows were among the first programs on television. And also the first to generate serious controversy. Accusations of impropriety and "fixed" episodes exploded, taking down a couple shows. While *Twenty-One* and *The $64,000 Question* didn't continue, others surfaced and the genre flourished. They survived those early accusations and have been a constant on the dial. In recent years, game shows like *Who Wants to Be a Millionaire?* and *The Weakest Link* became huge prime-time ratings successes, before settling into syndication alongside staples like *Wheel of Fortune* and *The Price Is Right*.

How much do you remember about these game shows?

1. Who was the first host of *Jeopardy?*
   a. Alex Trebek
   b. Bert Convy
   c. Allen Ludden
   d. Art Fleming

---

*host's question to contestants on *Who Wants to Be a Millionare?*

2. What did ABC change the name of *Who Wants to Be a Millionaire?* to when the prize was increased to $10 million?
   a. Celebrity Millionaire
   b. Super Millionaire
   c. Millionaire Deluxe
   d. Who Wants to Be a Multimillionaire?

3. Which was the first television show whose cast appeared on a celebrity-style version of *The Weakest Link*?
   a. *Survivor*
   b. *Third Watch*
   c. *The Brady Bunch*
   d. *Star Trek*

4. Who hosted *Wheel of Fortune* before Pat Sajak?
   a. Chuck Woolery
   b. Jack Barry
   c. Bill Cullen
   d. Bob Eubanks

5. What round followed the Lightning Round on *Password*?
   a. All or None
   b. Five in Twenty-Five
   c. Betting Word
   d. Final Password

6. How much can you win in cash playing Plinko on *The Price Is Right*?
   a. $5,000
   b. $10,000
   c. $25,000
   d. $50,000

7. How many rounds are there before the playoff round on *Pyramid*?
   a. Three
   b. Four
   c. Five
   d. Six

8. Which *M*A*S*H* cast member did not appear on *Match Game*, when the show was revived in the 1970s?
   a. McLean Stevenson
   b. Loretta Swit
   c. Gary Burghoff
   d. Mike Farrell

9. Who was not a host of *Family Feud*?
   a. Richard Dawson
   b. Louie Anderson
   c. Howie Mandel
   d. Richard Karn

10. On *Name That Tune*, what was the game called when contestants vied to be able to name a song in the least amount of notes?
    a. Melody Roulette
    b. Bid-a-Note
    c. Golden Medley
    d. Golden Medley Marathon

11. What were the worthless prizes on *Let's Make a Deal* called?
    a. Losers
    b. Zonks
    c. Junk
    d. Whammies

12. Who was the first celebrity to occupy the center square on *Hollywood Squares*?
    a. Charley Weaver
    b. Paul Lynde
    c. Wally Cox
    d. Ernest Borgnine

13. When *Concentration* resurfaced in the late 1980s as *Classic Concentration*, who was the host?
    a. Alex Trebek
    b. Chuck Woolery
    c. Ed MacMahon
    d. Hugh Downs

14. Who was the winner of the first *American Idol*?
    a. Kelly Clarkson
    b. Justin Guarini
    c. Clay Aiken
    d. Ruben Studdard

15. How much money were contestants playing for on *Win Ben Stein's Money*?
    a. $1,000
    b. $5,000
    c. $10,000
    d. $25,000

16. What was the first question worth on *The $64,000 Question*?
    a. $50
    b. $64
    c. $164
    d. $250

17. What game show staple got its start on *Twenty-One*?
    a. Lightning Round
    b. Isolation Booth
    c. Free Spin
    d. Double or Nothing

18. How much money did the top act receive on *The Gong Show*?
    a. $250
    b. $500
    c. $712.05
    d. $1,005.12

19. On *The Joker's Wild*, how much did a contestant need to win before proceeding to the bonus round?
    a. $500
    b. $1,000
    c. $2,500
    d. $5,000

20. On *To Tell the Truth*, who served as a guest host when Bud Collier was off?
    a. Merv Griffin
    b. Gene Rayburn
    c. John Cameron Swayze
    d. All of the Above

ANSWERS			
1. d	6. d	11. b	16. b
2. b	7. a	12. d	17. b
3. a	8. d	13. a	18. c
4. a	9. c	14. a	19. a
5. c	10. b	15. b	20. d

RICK AND LILY: WILL IT LAST?

hile soap operas are typically thought of as daytime fare, prime-time soaps have garnered huge ratings. Few shows (of any genre) on TV ever reached the popularity of *Dallas*, especially during the summer of 1980 when we all wondered, "Who shot J. R.?" Most prime-time soaps relied on the romance, more than the intrigue, while some have successfully blended the two.

How much do you remember about these night time soaps?

1. At the end of its series' run, who was in possession of Ewing Oil on *Dallas*?
   a. J. R. Ewing
   b. Bobby Ewing
   c. Cliff Barnes
   d. Jennifer Jansen

2. Who bought the house for Gary and Val on *Knots Landing*?
   a. Miss Ellie
   b. Jock
   c. J. R.
   d. Bobby

3. What did Teddy reveal after she got out of jail for displaying her nude photos in an exhibit on *Sisters*?
   a. She was pregnant
   b. She was gay
   c. She was running for mayor
   d. She was wanted for murder

4. What secret was Burt keeping that prevented him from making love to his wife, Mary, on *Soap*?
   a. He was an alien
   b. He had killed Peter
   c. He had killed her former husband
   d. He was in love with her sister, Jessica

5. Which character on *Dynasty*, after recovering from a bout of amnesia, saw a UFO?
   a. Blake Carrington
   b. Jeff Colby
   c. Fallon Carrington Colby
   d. Sammy Jo Dean

6. Who was Michael Mancini not married to on *Melrose Place*?
   a. Sydney
   b. Jane
   c. Kimberly
   d. Jo

7. Whose wedding came to a halt when the bride went into labor on *Beverly Hills 90210*?
   a. Nat and Joan's
   b. Brenda and Stuart's
   c. Dylan and Toni's
   d. Brandon and Kelly's

8. Where did Anna move to when she left *The OC*?
   a. Philadelphia
   b. Pittsburgh
   c. Cleveland
   d. Boston

9. Who got drunk and hit the groom at Robbie and Tina's wedding on *Providence*?
   a. Syd
   b. Joanie
   c. Jim
   d. Phil

10. Who killed the Lombardi's on *Mary Hartman, Mary Hartman*?
    a. Heather Hartman
    b. Davey Jessup
    c. Tom Hartman
    d. Raymond Larkin

11. On *The Colbys*, who ended up running off to New York to marry a Russian ballet dancer who defected for her?
    a. Francesca
    b. Monica
    c. Sable
    d. Bliss

12. Who accidentally burned down Edie's house on *Desperate Housewives*?
    a. Susan
    b. Lynette
    c. Bree
    d. Gabrielle

13. What surprise announcement does Lily make to Rick on the last episode of *Once and Again*?
    a. She's pregnant
    b. She's taking the syndication deal
    c. She's going with him to Australia
    d. She'll take the job and he'll go to Australia and they'll be together in a year

14. What surprise did Elliott reveal to Michael on the first episode of *thirtysomething*?
    a. He was leaving Nancy
    b. He had an affair with a former colleague
    c. He was quitting his job
    d. He isn't Ethan's father

15. Who was the only character that appeared in every episode of *Falcon Crest*?
    a. Lance Cumson
    b. Angela Channing
    c. Chase Gioberti
    d. Emma Channing

16. Who asked Jen if he could raise her baby, Amy, as Jen lay dying on the final episode of *Dawson's Creek*?
    a. Dawson
    b. Pacey
    c. Chris
    d. Jack

17. Who got married on the final episode of *Felicity*?
- **a.** Ben and Felicity
- **b.** Elena and Tracy
- **c.** Noel and Zoe
- **d.** Ben and Julie

18. Who was facing a murder trial when *Peyton Place* came to an end?
- **a.** Dr. Michael Rossi
- **b.** Rodney Harrington
- **c.** Steven Cord
- **d.** Eli Carson

19. Who did Kristen almost marry instead of Charlie on *Party of Five*?
- **a.** Michael
- **b.** Will
- **c.** Bailey
- **d.** Jake

20. Who had a Renaissance-themed wedding on *The Gilmore Girls*?
- **a.** Lorelai and Max
- **b.** Emily and Richard
- **c.** Lorelai and Rory
- **d.** Liz and T. J.

ANSWERS			
1. c	**6.** d	**11.** d	**16.** d
2. a	**7.** a	**12.** a	**17.** c
3. a	**8.** b	**13.** a	**18.** a
4. c	**9.** c	**14.** b	**19.** a
5. c	**10.** b	**15.** a	**20.** d

"Just sit right back and you'll hear a tale"*

There are so many television shows that can be conjured up by just a few notes of their memorable theme songs. Even the ones that didn't get played ad nauseam on the radio. Some gave us a musical history setting up the show, while others were just catchy tunes evoking the spirit of the program. How many of these toe-tapping TV themes do you remember?

1. Besides Gilligan, who was the only other castaway mentioned by their name in the theme to *Gilligan's Island*?
   a. Thurston Howell III
   b. Lovey
   c. Ginger
   d. Mary Ann

*from the theme song to *Gilligan's Island*

2. According to the theme from *Friends*, where are you always stuck?
   a. In a rut
   b. Out of luck
   c. In second gear
   d. In a dead-end job

3. What's the first line to the theme from *The Greatest American Hero*?
   a. "Look at what's happened to me"
   b. "Suddenly I'm up on top of the world"
   c. "It's like a light of a new day"
   d. "Believe it or not"

4. Before it got its own unique theme song, what 1950s song was used as the theme for *Happy Days*?
   a. "Blueberry Hill"
   b. "Rock and Roll Is Here to Stay"
   c. "Shake Rattle and Roll"
   d. "Rock around the Clock"

5. Who wrote "Best Friend" for *The Courtship of Eddie's Father*?
   a. Harry Nilsson
   b. Brian Wilson
   c. Tommy Boyce and Johnny Hart
   d. Paul Anka

6. What was the name of the theme to *The Partridge Family*?
   a. "I Think I Love You"
   b. "C'mon Get Happy"
   c. "Together (Havin' a Ball)"
   d. "I Really Want to Know You"

7. What was the opening line of *The Monkees*'s theme song?
   a. "Hey! Hey! We're the Monkees!"
   b. "We're the young generation"
   c. "Here we come"
   d. "Come watch us sing and play"

8. Who sang the theme to *Moonlighting*?
   a. Al Green
   b. Al Jarreau
   c. Smokey Robinson
   d. Barry White

9. What group was the singer a part of before he sang the theme to *Welcome Back, Kotter*?
   a. Lovin' Spoonful
   b. Peter, Paul, and Mary
   c. Turtles
   d. Beach Boys

10. According to the theme song for *The Brady Bunch*, what did the girls have in common with their mother?
    a. They were all happy
    b. They all had pretty smiles
    c. They all had blue eyes
    d. They all had hair of gold

11. On the theme to *Three's Company*, what comes after you're invited to "come and dance on our floor"?
    a. "We've been waiting for you"
    b. "Take a step that is new"
    c. "Come and knock on our door"
    d. "Laughter is calling for you"

12. According to the theme to *Alice*, what was her favorite sport?
    a. Football
    b. Singing
    c. Going through life with blinders on
    d. Kicking myself for nothing

13. What word had *Laverne and Shirley* never heard, according to their theme song?
    a. Difficult
    b. Impossible
    c. Unstoppable
    d. Hasenpfeffer

14. What's the first line of the theme song to *Cheers*?
    a. "Wouldn't you like to get away?"
    b. "Sometimes you want to go where everybody knows your name"
    c. "Making your way in the world today takes everything you've got"
    d. "You want to be where everyone knows your name"

15. What does she do with a "nothing day," according to the theme to *The Mary Tyler Moore Show*?
    a. "Make it all seem worthwhile"
    b. "Turn it around with her smile"
    c. "Turn the world on with her smile"
    d. "Take the town"

16. Who could we use a man like, again, according to the theme to *All in the Family*?
    a. Glenn Miller
    b. Herbert Hoover
    c. J. Edgar Hoover
    d. Milton Berle

17. Other than fish, what food is mentioned in the theme to *The Jeffersons*?
    a. Chicken
    b. Potatoes
    c. Beans
    d. Corn

18. Who wasn't mentioned in the theme to *Maude*?
    a. Lady Godiva
    b. Susan B. Anthony
    c. Joan of Arc
    d. Betsy Ross

19. Who sang the theme to *Family Ties* with Deniece Williams?
    a. Alan Thicke
    b. Johnny Mathis
    c. Neil Diamond
    d. Mel Torme

20. When *The Twilight Zone* was revived in the 1980s, who performed its theme song?
    a. REM
    b. Elvis Costello
    c. Grateful Dead
    d. Rolling Stones

ANSWERS			
1. d	6. b	11. b	16. b
2. c	7. c	12. d	17. c
3. a	8. b	13. b	18. b
4. d	9. a	14. c	19. b
5. a	10. d	15. a	20. c

A DIFFERENT KIND OF BAR

I n the early days of television drama, if the show wasn't about a doctor, the odds were good it involved the law. In the beginning, the shows dealt much more with the law, than with those that practiced it. More recently, we've gotten to know the lawyers much better. Little was ever revealed about *Perry Mason*'s personal life. By contrast, few details have been omitted from the personal lives of the characters on *L.A. Law*, *Ally McBeal*, and *Boston Legal*.

How much do you remember about these TV lawyers?

1. On *Law and Order*, what did Jack McCoy's father do for a living?
   a. Defense attorney
   b. Accountant
   c. Police officer
   d. Judge

2. What was unusual about *Perry Mason*'s client, Janice Barton, the woman accused of replacing her aunt's medicine with poison?
   a. She was Perry's sister
   b. Perry was found in contempt (the only time)
   c. Perry lost the case (the only time)
   d. She fired him (the only time)

3. Who did *L.A. Law*'s bigamist client (who had eleven wives) teach "The Venus Butterfly" sexual maneuver to?
   a. Arnie Becker
   b. Stuart Markowtiz
   c. Michael Kuzak
   d. Ann Kelsey

4. In the first season of *Dharma and Greg*, what job does Greg get when he follows Dharma's advice and quits law to "follow his bliss"?
   a. Short order cook
   b. Caddy
   c. Hairdresser
   d. House painter

5. How did Judge Stone decide his first case on *Night Court*?
   a. Rock, paper, and scissors
   b. Had the parties guess what number he was thinking of
   c. Hi-lo
   d. Flipped a coin

6. Who did Amy hire as her clerk when she was transferred to Criminal Court on *Judging Amy*?
   a. Donna
   b. Gillian
   c. Victor
   d. Lisa

7. When Don Knotts's character, Ace, moved in next door to *Matlock*, what crime was he (Ace) charged with, prompting Matlock to defend him?
   a. Murdering a used car salesman
   b. Murdering his ex-wife
   c. Murdering his boss
   d. Murdering a gay tenant in his apartment complex

8. How did Ellenor meet George Vogelman, the podiatrist that showed up at the offices of *The Practice* with a severed head in his medical bag?
   a. He was her doctor
   b. He was her neighbor
   c. He answered her personal ad
   d. He was moving his office into their building and met her on the elevator

9. Who was the only member of the law firm to be made a partner of Cage and Fish on *Ally McBeal*?
   a. Ally McBeal
   b. Billy Thomas
   c. Ling Woo
   d. Nelle Porter

10. Why did Alan Shore's client want to sue the touring company of *Annie* on *Boston Legal*?
    a. They refused to sell her tickets
    b. They refused to refund her tickets for a cancelled performance
    c. They didn't select her child to star because she's black
    d. They didn't select her child to star because he's a boy

11. On *Family Law*, who played Randi King's cousin Marcie, who was accused of abusing her mother who was suffering from Alzheimer's?
    a. Annie Potts
    b. Delta Burke
    c. Jean Smart
    d. Alice Ghostley

12. Why did Warren need Ed Stevens legal help on *Ed*?
    a. Jessica broke their date "contract"
    b. He was arrested for underage drinking
    c. He was arrested for bringing a keg to a party and contributing to an accident
    d. He was arrested for pulling the fire alarm at school

13. What was Mac's first name on *JAG*?
    a. Michelle
    b. Margaret
    c. Susan
    d. Sarah

14. When Bernstein saved Joyce from an escaped prisoner on *Hill Street Blues*, what secret did he confess to her?
    a. He had a crush on her
    b. He was her half-brother
    c. He was going to law school at night
    d. The escaped prisoner was his brother

15. On *The Paper Chase*, where did Hart pick up a part-time job while in law school?
    a. The law library
    b. In Kingsfield's office as a clerk
    c. Ernie's Burgers
    d. Ernie's Pizza

16. Who played Mr. Stein, the senior partner of Will's firm, on *Will and Grace*?
    a. Gregory Hines
    b. Gene Wilder
    c. Richard Pryor
    d. Mel Brooks

17. What's the name of Sandy's restaurant on *The OC*?
    a. The OC
    b. Lighthouse
    c. Wharf
    d. J & S

18. Where did Oliver not want to be listed as an attorney on *Green Acres*?
    a. The new Hooterville phone book
    b. Haney's Hooterville Job Guide
    c. Sam Drucker's new billboard
    d. The Cannonball's printed schedule

19. Who was the lawyer frequently hired by *The Simpsons*?
    a. Troy McClure
    b. Lionel Hutz
    c. Clancy Wiggum
    d. Joe Quimby

20. How was *Chicago Hope*'s legal counsel, Alan Birch, killed off?
    a. Cancer
    b. Stroke
    c. Botched appendix operation
    d. Shot on the streets of Chicago

ANSWERS

1. c	**6.** a	**11.** b	**16.** b
2. c	**7.** a	**12.** c	**17.** b
3. b	**8.** c	**13.** d	**18.** a
4. a	**9.** a	**14.** a	**19.** b
5. d	**10.** c	**15.** d	**20.** d

$200 PER DAY PLUS EXPENSES

Private investigators bridged the gap between lawyers and cops on television. They gave you a nontraditional hero, usually on the right side of the law, but without the security (or authority) of the police or the propriety (or decorum) of lawyers. The private eyes ran the gamut, from those barely making ends meet, like James Garner's character on *The Rockford Files*, to those that were a little more secure, like the wealthy couple on *Hart to Hart*.

How much do you remember about these TV private investigators?

1. What did Thomas Magnum's unseen boss, Robin Masters, do for a living on *Magnum, P.I.*?
   a. CIA operative
   b. Oil company executive
   c. Writer
   d. Ambassador to an unnamed foreign country

2. What crime was Jim Rockford in prison for (and later pardoned for) on *The Rockford Files*?
   a. Armed robbery
   b. Murder
   c. Embezzlement
   d. Stock fraud

3. Who was Laura Holt's partner, before *Remington Steele* first walked through the doors of her agency?
   a. Murphy Michaels
   b. Michael Murphy
   c. Martin Murphy
   d. Murphy Martin

4. Who lived closest to their office, in an apartment in the back, on *Simon and Simon*?
   a. A. J. Simon
   b. Rick Simon
   c. Myron Fowler
   d. Downtown Brown

5. What was the name of Maddie's agency on *Moonlighting*?
   a. Moon Dance
   b. Moon Flower
   c. Blue Moon
   d. Full Moon

6. What nickname did Dan Tanna use to refer to his millionaire boss, Philip Roth, on *Vega$*?
   a. Chips
   b. Phyllis
   c. Pip
   d. Slick

7. What was *Mannix*'s first name?
   a. Joe
   b. Jack
   c. Jim
   d. Jan

8. On the first episode of *Barnaby Jones*, who crossed over from their series to help Jones track down the person that killed his son?
   a. Kojak
   b. Cannon
   c. Mannix
   d. Toma

9. Who made, planted, and detonated the car bomb that killed *Monk*'s wife, Trudy?
   a. Dale the Whale
   b. Warrick Tennyson
   c. Monica Waters
   d. Dwight Ellison

10. In what city was *Spenser for Hire* based?
    a. New York City
    b. Philadelphia
    c. Boston
    d. Chicago

11. Who was the former cop on *Switch*?
    a. Frank McBride
    b. Pete Ryan
    c. Pete McBride
    d. Frank Ryan

12. On *Charlie's Angels*, who was kidnapped on the episode that introduced Kris Munroe, played by Cheryl Ladd?
   a. Bosley
   b. Jill
   c. Kelly
   d. Charlie

13. What did *Cannon* do in almost every episode?
   a. Wreck his car
   b. Cook a gourmet meal
   c. Not fire a single shot
   d. All of the above

14. What 1970s P.I. does Mark Sloan help to solve a twenty-five-year-old murder on *Diagnosis Murder*?
   a. Cannon
   b. Barnaby Jones
   c. Mannix
   d. Toma

15. Who played Father Dowling's evil brother Blaine on the *Father Dowling Mysteries*?
   a. Eddie Albert
   b. Dick Van Dyke
   c. Ron Howard
   d. Tom Bosley

16. What was unusual about Jonathan and Jennifer's relationship on *Hart to Hart*?
   a. They weren't really married
   b. They met and got engaged on the same day
   c. They met on a blind date in Paris
   d. They're marriage was arranged by their parents

17. Who did "The Face" turn out to be on *Mickey Spillane's Mike Hammer*?
    a. Hammer's sister
    b. Hammer's ex-wife
    c. Writer chronicling Hammer's adventures
    d. Velda

18. What was the name of the jazz club that was the favorite hangout for *Peter Gunn*?
    a. Mother's Jazz Club
    b. Daddy's Jazz Club
    c. Edie's Jazz Club
    d. Emmett's Jazz Club

19. Which restaurant, where Kookie served as a parking lot attendant, was next door to *77 Sunset Strip*?
    a. Renaldo's
    b. Mario's
    c. Dino's
    d. Antonio's

20. Who was *The Equalizer*'s partner when he was a British agent working for The Company?
    a. Chaos
    b. Control
    c. Chief
    d. Cannon

ANSWERS			
1. c	**6.** d	**11.** a	**16.** b
2. a	**7.** a	**12.** d	**17.** c
3. a	**8.** b	**13.** d	**18.** a
4. a	**9.** b	**14.** c	**19.** c
5. c	**10.** c	**15.** d	**20.** b

"PEOPLE LET ME TELL YOU 'BOUT MY BEST FRIEND"*

Even though the censors were much more strict in the early days of television, the idea of single parents was still around, even then. The reasons were different, of course. The death of a spouse was typically the reason a character was raising a child on their own—as with *The Courtship of Eddie's Father*, *The Andy Griffith Show*, and *Petticoat Junction*. More recently, divorce played a more prominent role—as in *Two and a Half Men* and *Arrested Development*. And an idea that would have turned those early censors on their heads—some characters chose to have babies even though they weren't married! *Ally McBeal* and *Murphy Brown* both made headlines with those stories.

How much do you remember about these single TV parents and their shows?

---

*from the theme song to *The Courtship of Eddie's Father*

1. What was Eddie's father's name on *The Courtship of Eddie's Father*?
   a. Tom Corbett
   b. Edward Corbett
   c. Tom Livingston
   d. Tom Rickles

2. How did Andy Taylor meet Helen Crump on *The Andy Griffith Show*?
   a. She was the new pharmacist
   b. She was Floyd's new manicurist
   c. She was Opie's teacher
   d. She was a member of Aunt Bee's bingo club

3. Who told Uncle Bill that Cissy left Buffy and Jody alone when she went off to Dartmouth with Gregg on *Family Affair*?
   a. Buffy
   b. Jody
   c. Mr. French
   d. Cissy

4. Who was the father of Murphy's baby, Avery, on *Murphy Brown*?
   a. Peter Hunt
   b. Jake Lowenstein
   c. Eldin Bernecky
   d. Jerry Gold

5. How did Vicki discover that Captain Stubing was her father on *Love Boat*?
   a. She read it in her mother's diary
   b. Her mother told her just before she died
   c. Her aunt told her
   d. She overheard Captain Stubing telling Julie

6. Why did all the kids in Jake's class stop picking on Charlie when he was left alone with them on *Two and a Half Men*?
   a. He asked them for advice on women
   b. He threatened to get them extra homework
   c. He gave them candy
   d. Jake told them Charlie wrote a cereal jingle

7. Who finally confessed their twenty-five-year secret passion for Kate on *Petticoat Junction*?
   a. Fred Ziffel
   b. Sam Drucker
   c. Homer Bedloe
   d. Steve Elliott

8. What was Lamont's mother's name, who died many years before on *Sanford and Son*?
   a. Elizabeth
   b. Elenore
   c. Ellen
   d. Esther

9. In the first episode of *Arrested Development*, where was Michael Bluth going to take his son, George-Michael, to start their new lives?
   a. Florida
   b. Texas
   c. Colorado
   d. Arizona

10. Who was the father of Carol Hathaway's twins on *ER*?
    a. Doug Ross
    b. Mark Greene
    c. John "Tag" Taglieri
    d. Ray "Shep" Shepard

11. Who was Margie's neighbor, whom she was frequently scheming with to control her father, on *My Little Margie*?
    a. Roberta
    b. Mrs. Odetts
    c. Mrs. Honeywell
    d. Charlie

12. What unusual trait did Adam, Hoss, and Little Joe (Ben Cartwright's songs) all have in common on *Bonanza*?
    a. They were all left-handed
    b. Their middle names were the same: Benjamin
    c. They all had different mothers
    d. They all had served in the army during the Civil War

13. Who was the only one of the Douglas family that didn't get married on *My Three Sons*?
    a. Robbie
    b. Chip
    c. Ernie
    d. Steve

14. When *Flipper* returned to TV in the 1990s, other than the dolphin, what character from the original series also returned?
    a. Porter Ricks
    b. Bud Ricks
    c. Sandy Ricks
    d. Ulla Norstrand

15. On *Blossom*, what do the kids try to keep Nick from seeing?
    a. Joey's tattoo
    b. The car Anthony wrecked
    c. Blossom's report card
    d. Nick's divorce papers

16. When Grace met Juan (*Jack and Bobby*'s father), what was he doing for a living?
   a. Busboy
   b. Waiter
   c. Archeologist
   d. College professor

17. How old was Lorelai when she got pregnant with Rory on *Gilmore Girls*?
   a. 21
   b. 20
   c. 18
   d. 16

18. Shortly after Paul's death, what did Cate encourage Rory to do that his father would have wanted on *8 Simple Rules*?
   a. To write for the school paper
   b. To study harder in school
   c. To try out for the football team
   d. To try out for the basketball team

19. After Mindy's father sold the music store, what did he do for a living on *Mork and Mindy*?
   a. Orchestra conductor
   b. Radio host
   c. Concert violinist
   d. Agent for a young opera singer

20. After winning custody of Wendy, what happened when Jodie went to therapy on *Soap*?
   a. He got amnesia
   b. He thought he was an old Jewish man
   c. He thought he was a woman
   d. He thought he was an old Jewish woman

ANSWERS

1.	a	**6.**	d	**11.**	b	**16.**	a
2.	c	**7.**	b	**12.**	c	**17.**	d
3.	d	**8.**	a	**13.**	c	**18.**	d
4.	b	**9.**	d	**14.**	b	**19.**	a
5.	a	**10.**	a	**15.**	d	**20.**	b

FACING REALITY

Many claim that Reality TV is a recent phenomenon, but that's hardly the case. As with most genres, it's merely the hot property at the moment—just as procedural law enforcement shows continue to gain in popularity now. While MTV's *Real World* may have led to *Survivor*, neither may have come about without *Candid Camera*. The only difference is that, early on, those appearing on camera may not have known they were being filmed. Changes in the law have kept that from recurring.

How much do you remember about these Reality shows?

1. Where did the first season of *Survivor* take place?
   a. Australia
   b. Thailand
   c. Borneo
   d. Marquesas

2. Who won the first celebrity edition of *Fear Factor*?
   a. Donny Osmond
   b. Coolio
   c. David Hasselhoff
   d. Kelly Preston

3. Other than Allen Funt, who else appeared as a host or cohost on *Candid Camera*?
   a. Dom DeLuise
   b. Suzanne Somers
   c. Arthur Godfrey
   d. All of the above

4. What city is the only one to have been the setting for *The Real World* twice?
   a. London
   b. Chicago
   c. New York
   d. Los Angeles

5. Before moving the show to New York, where did *Queer Eye for the Straight Guy* originally take place?
   a. Boston
   b. Philadelphia
   c. Baltimore
   d. Chicago

6. On *Who Wants To Marry My Dad?*, which of the contestants was actually Marty's (the dad's) sister-in-law?
   a. Layne
   b. Tina
   c. Lolo
   d. Sarah

7. What did the second *Joe Millionaire* actually do for a living?
   a. Video store clerk
   b. Rodeo cowboy
   c. Car mechanic
   d. Dairy assistant manager

8. What prize did viewers of *Real People* win when one of their photos was used on the show?
    a. *Real People* T-shirt
    b. *Real People* home game
    c. *Real People* refrigerator magnet
    d. Autographed picture of Sarah Purcell

9. Which of the following is not one of the specialists used on *The Swan*?
    a. Laser Eye Surgeon
    b. Nutritionalist
    c. Fitness trainer
    d. Dermatologist

10. What does the final contestant, the only one not voted out of the house, win on *Big Brother*?
    a. $100,000
    b. $250,000
    c. $500,000
    d. $1,000,000

11. Which couple from *The Bachelor* or *The Bachelorette* actually got married?
    a. Trista and Ryan
    b. Alex and Amanda
    c. Aaron and Helene
    d. All of the above

12. On the first season of *The Apprentice*, what did the men name their company?
    a. Protégé
    b. Versacorp
    c. Apex
    d. Mosaic

13. Who was the announcer for the pilot of *COPS*?
    a. Robert Blake
    b. Telly Sevalas
    c. Burt Lancaster
    d. Kirk Douglas

14. What is the budget couples are given on *Trading Spaces*?
    a. $500
    b. $1,000
    c. $2,500
    d. $5,000

15. What is the cash prize for the winner of *The Biggest Loser*?
    a. $100,000
    b. $250,000
    c. $500,000
    d. $1,000,000

16. How long did the Bowler family have to live in *1900 House* on the first of PBS's "House" series?
    a. One month
    b. Three months
    c. Six months
    d. One year

17. What does the winning team on *The Amazing Race* receive?
    a. $100,000
    b. $250,000
    c. $500,000
    d. $1,000,000

18. Who won on the final season of *Celebrity Mole* (which took place in Yucatan)?
    a. Stephen Baldwin
    b. Dennis Rodman
    c. Tracey Gold
    d. Mark Curry

19. When *America's Funniest Home Videos* began, what did the weekly first prize winner receive?
    a. $1,000
    b. $2,500
    c. $5,000
    d. $10,000

20. What's the hotline number for *America's Most Wanted*?
    a. 1-800-CRIME-TV
    b. 1-800-MWANTED
    c. 1-800-FIGHT-BK
    d. 1-800-USA-MOST

ANSWERS

1. c	6. c	11. a	16. b
2. b	7. b	12. b	17. d
3. d	8. a	13. c	18. b
4. c	9. b	14. b	19. d
5. a	10. c	15. b	20. a

SHOWS ABOUT NOTHING

Jerry Seinfeld's show wasn't really about nothing. It often had many clever plotlines, deftly converging by the end of the show. Often, his observances were similar to his stand-up, and sometimes the episodes were built around that. He wasn't the first.

Television often mined its talent from comedy clubs and, earlier, from radio and vaudeville. From Jackie Gleason, Sid Caesar, and Burns and Allen, programs were built around the performers. More recently, the same has happened with comedians like Tim Allen, Ray Romano, and Bernie Mac.

How much about these shows featuring stand-up comedians do you remember?

1. What was the name of Kotter's agent, who allowed Gabe Kaplan to go full circle by having his character take a shot at stand-up comedy on *Welcome Back, Kotter*?
   a. Pete
   b. Sam
   c. Nick
   d. George

2. On *The George Burns and Gracie Allen Show*, who was the neighbor with which Gracie concocted most of her schemes?
   a. Bonnie Sue McAfee
   b. Blanche Morton
   c. Emily Vanderlip
   d. Ethel Mertz

3. While the majority of the pilot episode of *The Cosby Show* came directly from Bill Cosby's stand-up, what on the show specifically matched Cosby's real life?
   a. He had four daughters and one son
   b. He graduated from medical school
   c. His wife is a lawyer
   d. All of the above

4. While waiting for Jerry backstage at *The Tonight Show*, who did George pitch an idea to on *Seinfeld*?
   a. Jose Carrera
   b. Alex Trebek
   c. Corbin Bernsen
   d. Jimmy Smits

5. How did Tim try to cheat in a lawn mower race against Bob Villa on *Home Improvement*?
   a. Rebuilt his mower with a part from a Chinese helicopter
   b. Rebuilt his mower with a part from an army tank
   c. Rebuilt it with help from Michael Andretti
   d. Rebuilt it with help from a group of NASA astronauts

6. On a clip show, which TV mom did not visit *Roseanne* as part of the "Sitcom Moms Welcome Wagon"?
   a. Isabel Sanford
   b. June Lockhart
   c. Barbara Billingsley
   d. Florence Henderson

7. When Doug was assigned a new delivery route on *King of Queens*, what problem did he run into?
   a. His ex-girlfriend is on the route
   b. A new customer looks just like Carrie
   c. A new customer always answers the door in nothing but a towel
   d. A new customer has no parking or loading zones all around his business

8. Who came up with the name "Buzz Beer" on *The Drew Carey Show*?
   a. Drew
   b. Oswald
   c. Kate
   d. Lewis

9. What was Robert Hartley's job in *The Bob Newhart Show*?
   a. Psychiatrist
   b. Psychologist
   c. Writer
   d. Innkeeper

10. What comedian made a rare sitcom appearance on *Mork and Mindy* as the leader of a seminar called ERK (Ellsworth Revitalization Konditioning)?
    a. Jay Leno
    b. Johnny Carson
    c. Ed McMahon
    d. David Letterman

11. What was Grace's last name on *Grace under Fire*?
    a. Kelly
    b. Norton
    c. Swoboda
    d. Autry

12. Before being renamed *Ellen*, what was Ellen DeGeneres'
    show's original name?
    a. *Friends*
    b. *Pals*
    c. *These Friends of Mine*
    d. *Me and My Friends*

13. When *The Jeff Foxworthy Show* moved from ABC to NBC, the
    setting for the show changed from Indiana to where?
    a. New Orleans
    b. Atlanta
    c. Houston
    d. Savannah

14. Which of the following does English comedian Rowan
    Atkinson not do on the first episode of *Mr. Bean*?
    a. Cheat on an exam
    b. Go to the beach
    c. Go to the library
    d. Try to stay awake at church

15. On *The Steve Harvey Show*, what does Steve Hightower do for
    a living?
    a. High school principal
    b. High school music teacher
    c. High school guidance counselor
    d. High school English teacher

16. What was Norm Henderson's career before he was sen-
    tenced to work as a social worker on *Norm*?
    a. Professional hockey player
    b. Professional football player
    c. Professional basketball player
    d. Professional baseball player

17. When Ray got an honorary doctorate, who did he forget to mention in his acceptance speech on *Everybody Loves Raymond*?
    a. Debra
    b. Frank
    c. Marie
    d. Robert

18. In the series finale for Martin Lawrence's sitcom *Martin*, where was Martin Payne moving?
    a. Chicago
    b. Detroit
    c. Los Angeles
    d. New York

19. Why did Bernie and Vanessa end up with his sister's kids on *The Bernie Mac Show*?
    a. She was killed in a car accident
    b. She was in jail
    c. She was in rehab
    d. She left them and ran off with her coworker

20. What catch phrase from Freddie Prinze's stand-up act became a staple of his show *Chico and the Man*?
    a. What do you mean?
    b. Who me?
    c. I'm not doing that
    d. It's not my job

ANSWERS			
1. a	6. d	11. a	16. a
2. b	7. c	12. c	17. a
3. a	8. b	13. b	18. c
4. c	9. b	14. c	19. b
5. a	10. d	15. b	20. d

"LIVE FROM NEW YORK, IT'S SATURDAY NIGHT"

Few programs have had the effect on popular culture as *Saturday Night Live* has. While it's endured numerous cast changes, the show has consistently launched the careers of many comedic stars. Popular characters from the show have appeared in movies, sometimes successfully and sometimes not.

Still, the show has lasted for over thirty seasons. And thrived, despite losing many of its biggest stars.

How much do you remember about *Saturday Night Live*?

1. Where did the Coneheads claim to be from?
   a. Sweden
   b. Australia
   c. France
   d. Paraguay

2. What city was home to Wayne's World?
   a. Indianapolis, Indiana
   b. Aurora, Illinois
   c. Terra Haute, Indiana
   d. Bloomington, Illinois

3. Who was the first anchor of Weekend Update?
   a. Jane Curtain
   b. Dan Aykroyd
   c. Chevy Chase
   d. Bill Murray

4. Who was the guest host the night Lorne Michaels made his appeal to the Beatles to appear?
   a. Raquel Welch
   b. George Carlin
   c. Madeline Kahn
   d. Elliott Gould

5. What was the name of the liar character that Jon Lovitz played?
   a. Tommy Findley
   b. Tommy Foster
   c. Tommy Flannagan
   d. Tommy Finnegan

6. What sport did the Spartan Cheerleaders cheer for?
   a. Beach volleyball
   b. Chess
   c. Wrestling
   d. All of the above

7. What fake MTV show was "Goatboy" the host of?
   a. *Remember the '80s*
   b. *Remember the '90s*
   c. *Science Experiments of the Rich and Famous*
   d. *Pseudo Celebrity Cribs*

8. At the beginning of "Brain Fellow's Safari Planet," what kind of education does the announcer claim Brian has?
   a. None
   b. Junior College
   c. Junior High
   d. Sixth Grade

9. What was the name of Tim Meadows's "Ladies' Man"?
   a. Lester Phelps
   b. Leon Phelps
   c. Leon Phillips
   d. Lonnie Phillips

10. Which scenario was the first appearance for John Belushi's Samurai character?
    a. Samurai Delicatessen
    b. Samurai Dry Cleaner
    c. Samurai Hotel
    d. Samurai Psychiatrist

11. What was the segment with Dana Carvey's "Church Lady" called?
    a. Church Talk
    b. Church Chat
    c. Church Minutes
    d. Church Bulletin

12. Where the "wild and crazy" Festrunk brothers supposed to be from?
    a. France
    b. Czecholslavakia
    c. Yugoslavia
    d. Poland

13. Who was arrested for shooting Buckwheat?
    a. Alfalfa
    b. Spanky
    c. John David Stutts
    d. Jonathan Alan Thomas

14. Who played Nick Burns, the computer guy?
    a. Will Ferrell
    b. Jimmy Fallon
    c. Darrell Hammond
    d. Chris Kattan

15. In the first couple appearances of Chevy Chase's Land Shark, who played the sheriff that was trying to catch him?
    a. Bill Murray
    b. John Belushi
    c. Garrett Morris
    d. Dan Aykroyd

16. Who was Mr. Bill's dog?
    a. Spot
    b. Rover
    c. Fido
    d. Mr. Bill didn't have a dog; he had a cat

17. Who played Franz to Dana Carvey's Hans?
    a. Dennis Miller
    b. Kevin Nealon
    c. Phil Hartman
    d. Mike Myers

18. Who was anchor of Weekend Update for the longest?
   a. Dennis Miller
   b. Kevin Nealon
   c. Jane Curtain
   d. Norm MacDonald

19. Who was Mister Robinson's new neighbor, who didn't like him playing the drums?
   a. Ringo Starr
   b. Sylvester Stallone
   c. Mr. T
   d. Christopher Reeve

20. What was Billy Crystal's character Fernando's credo on "Fernando's Hideaway"?
   a. It is better to look good than to feel good
   b. It is better to look marvelous than to feel marvelous
   c. It is good to look better than you feel
   d. It feels good to look marvelous

ANSWERS			
1. c	**6.** d	**11.** b	**16.** a
2. b	**7.** a	**12.** b	**17.** b
3. c	**8.** d	**13.** c	**18.** a
4. a	**9.** b	**14.** b	**19.** c
5. c	**10.** c	**15.** d	**20.** a

ANOTHER THREE-HOUR CRUISE?

Almost as soon as television was old enough, it began revisiting itself. Reunion shows cropped up, allowing us to check in on some of our favorite characters years after their shows had left the air—giving us updates on Jim Rockford, the Brady family, and Gilligan.

Other times, writers would pay homage to some of their favorites by allowing characters from old shows to appear in a new program. The best example of this was probably on *Mad About You* when Paul Buchman worked on a documentary about Alan Brady, the character who's show was the focus of *The Dick Van Dyke Show*.

And lastly, some programs have just been redone, updated for the new generation, sometimes bringing along old characters, as when Johnny Fever visited *The New WKRP in Cincinnati*, and sometimes simply starting with a clean slate, as with *Flipper* and *Dragnet*.

How much do you remember about these reunion shows?

1. Who was the only member of the Seaver family, other than Jason, who wanted the family's house to be sold on *Growing Pains: The Return of the Seavers*?
   a. Mike
   b. Carol
   c. Ben
   d. Maggie

2. When Mary Richards and Rhoda Morganstern returned to TV on *Mary and Rhoda*, what did Mary now do for a living?
   a. Worked for ABC news as a producer
   b. Worked for WJM again, this time as news director
   c. Was running for political office
   d. Was unemployed

3. When Andy Taylor returned to Mayberry in 1986, who was running for sheriff?
   a. Barney Fife
   b. Opie Taylor
   c. Goober Pyle
   d. Warren Ferguson

4. Who did Michael Kuzak have to face in court when *L.A. Law*'s *Return to Justice* aired in 2002?
   a. Grace Van Owen
   b. Leland MacKenzie
   c. Victor Sifuentes
   d. Roxanne Melman

5. Who was missing from *The Facts of Life Reunion*?
   a. Blair
   b. Jo
   c. Natalie
   d. Tootie

6. Who no longer worked at the station when *The New WKRP in Cincinnati* surfaced in 1991?
   a. Herb Tarlek
   b. Les Nessman
   c. Arthur Carlson
   d. Venus Flytrap

7. In the second *Dallas*'s reunion, *War of the Ewings*, who shot J. R.?
   a. Sue Ellen
   b. Bobby Ewing
   c. Ray Krebbs
   d. Peter Ellington

8. A different actor played whose part in the first *I Dream of Jeannie* reunion—*I Dream of Jeannie 15 Years Later*?
   a. Tony Nelson
   b. Jeannie
   c. Roger Healey
   d. Dr. Bellows

9. Whose role was recast on the first *Gilligan's Island* reunion, *Rescue from Gilligan's Island*?
   a. Lovey Howell
   b. Ginger Grant
   c. Mary Ann Summers
   d. Professor Roy Hinkley

10. Whose son is Jim Rockford's godson, which the fourth *Rockford Files*'s reunion, *Godfather Knows Best*, was largely about?
    a. Rocky's
    b. Becker's
    c. Angel's
    d. Gus's

11. When Ponch and Jon returned in *CHiPs 99*, who was captain?
    a. Ponch
    b. Jon
    c. Bruce
    d. Getraer

12. On *Halloween with the Addams Family*, who does Gomez's brother Pancho say distributes gifts on Halloween?
    a. Cousin Shy
    b. Cousin Quincy
    c. Countess Dracula
    d. Great Pumpkin

13. In their 1997 reunion, which old song did the Monkees perform as part of a medley?
    a. "Last Train to Clarksville"
    b. "I'm a Believer"
    c. "Words"
    d. All of the above

14. While many original cast members returned for *The Dick Van Dyke Show Revisited*, what comedian introduced the show?
    a. Drew Carey
    b. Ray Romano
    c. Paul Reiser
    d. Jerry Seinfeld

15. On the second *Six Million Dollar Man/Bionic Woman* reunion, *The Bionic Showdown*, who guest-starred as a wheelchair-bound woman about to become the new bionic woman?
    a. Demi Moore
    b. Sandra Bullock
    c. Julia Roberts
    d. Sharon Stone

16. While it had only been three years since the show left the air, what event brought the cast of *Beverly Hills 90210* back?
    a. Donna and David's wedding
    b. The birth of Donna and David's first child
    c. Their fifth high school reunion
    d. Their tenth high school reunion

17. Which two of the Brady kids got married in a double wedding, which was an attempt at starting a new series featuring the newlyweds?
    a. Marcia and Jan
    b. Jan and Cindy
    c. Marcia and Greg
    d. Jan and Peter

18. In the first *Gunsmoke* reunion, *Return to Dodge*, what character from the original series did not return?
    a. Marshal Dillon
    b. Miss Kitty
    c. Newly O'Brien
    d. Chester Goode

19. On *Laverne and Shirley Together Again*, what show were the two trying to get parts on?
    a. *Jeopardy*
    b. *Wheel of Fortune*
    c. *You Bet Your Life*
    d. *Survivor*-type reality show

20. What does Emily attribute Bob's dream of being a Vermont innkeeper to on *The Bob Newhart Show* finale of *Newhart*?
    a. Japanese food before bed
    b. Scary movie before bed
    c. Drinking with Jerry and his cousins (both named Harold) before bed
    d. Watching bad TV sitcoms before bed

ANSWERS

1. c	**6.** d	**11.** b	**16.** d
2. d	**7.** d	**12.** a	**17.** a
3. a	**8.** a	**13.** d	**18.** d
4. a	**9.** b	**14.** b	**19.** d
5. b	**10.** b	**15.** b	**20.** a

"IT HAPPENED TO TINY TIM"*

Many special occasions have been celebrated on TV shows, but few events have shown up on more programs than the Christmas episode. In fact, it would be easier to list the shows that didn't have at least one holiday-themed episode. *I Dream of Jeannie* didn't have one. None of the *Star Treks* had one, either. And there may be one or two others.

For the most part, though, our favorite characters on our favorite shows were doing the same things we were doing in December. *Murphy Brown* and *Frasier* both tried to find that singular hot toy of the season for their kids. Hazel, Homer Simpson, and *The Beverly Hillbillies* all got seasonal jobs to earn extra money for presents. And the real Santa visited the Ricardos, *The Addams Family*, and the castaways of *Gilligan's Island*.

How much do you remember about these shows' Christmas episodes?

---

*Bart from the first episode of *The Simpsons*: "If TV has taught me anything, it's that miracles happen to poor kids at Christmas. It happened to Tiny Tim. It happened to Charlie Brown. It happened to the Smurfs. And it's gonna happen to us!"

1. What second job did Homer get on *The Simpsons*'s first episode to raise extra money for Christmas gifts for his family?
   a. Pin-setter at bowling alley
   b. Mascot for baseball team
   c. Concert security
   d. Department store Santa

2. Who was *Frasier*'s cohost for the annual Christmas parade?
   a. Roz
   b. Dr. Mary
   c. Bulldog
   d. Niles

3. When *Murphy Brown* takes in a trio of abandoned children one Christmas, what does she discover they asked Santa to bring her?
   a. A car
   b. A husband
   c. A pony
   d. A million jillion dollars

4. On *Married . . . with Children*, why was the mall Santa late?
   a. His parachute didn't open and he crashed into the Bundy's yard
   b. Al got into a fight with him and knocked him out
   c. Al took him to a bar and they both got drunk
   d. He was on a date with Kelly

5. When he can't find a Santa suit, what costume does Ross get to wear for Ben on *Friends*?
   a. Easter Bunny
   b. Superman
   c. Armadillo
   d. Anteater

6. What did Samantha do on *Bewitched* to prove to Michael that there really is a Santa Claus?
   a. Showed him his future
   b. Showed him what Santa's done in the past
   c. Took him to a department store to meet Santa
   d. Took him to the North Pole to meet Santa

7. On *Green Acres*, what did Mr. Haney tell Oliver he had to get a permit for?
   a. Putting up his Christmas lights
   b. Chopping down a tree on his own property
   c. Putting decorations on his roof
   d. Having a Christmas party

8. Who broke into Bree's house and decorated it with lights, a tree, and stockings on *Desperate Housewives*?
   a. Zack Young
   b. Rex Van de Camp
   c. Mike Delfino
   d. Susan Mayer

9. When Doug got a Christmas bonus, what did he and Carrie decide to do with it on *King of Queens*?
   a. Put it in the bank
   b. Buy a new car
   c. Buy a present for Arthur
   d. Buy an Internet stock

10. Who found a baby left in their home on *Moonlighting*?
   a. Maddie Hayes
   b. David Addison
   c. Agnes DiPesto
   d. Herbert Viola

11. Who worked as a department store Santa on *Seinfeld*?
    a. George
    b. Kramer
    c. Jerry
    d. Elaine

12. On the first season of *Spin City*, who played the City Hall Santa?
    a. Mike
    b. Carter
    c. Paul
    d. Stuart

13. Who routinely beat Tim in the Christmas decorating contest on *Home Improvement*?
    a. Al Boreland
    b. Bob Villa
    c. Doc Johnson
    d. Wilson

14. How did Louie get his brother to take their mother on a Christmas vacation on *Taxi*?
    a. Beat him in a high stakes hand of poker
    b. Got Alex to beat him in a high stakes hand of poker
    c. Got Bobby to beat him in a high stakes hand of poker
    d. Got Elaine to beat him in a high stakes hand of poker

15. Where were the Tanners heading for the holidays when they got snowed in at an airport on *Full House*?
    a. San Francisco
    b. New York
    c. Colorado
    d. Utah

16. Who got stuck in the chimney on *The Addams Family*?
    a. Lurch
    b. Cousin Itt
    c. Uncle Fester
    d. Santa

17. While everyone was worried she was spending Christmas alone, where was Jennifer actually going to spend the holiday on *WKRP in Cincinnati*?
    a. North Pole
    b. Las Vegas
    c. Aspen
    d. Bethlehem

18. What did Kevin and Wayne try to convince their father to buy for Christmas on *The Wonder Years*?
    a. New car
    b. Dog
    c. Pool table
    d. Color television

19. Who came back to the newsroom to keep Mary company when she had to work alone on Christmas Eve on *The Mary Tyler Moore Show*?
    a. Lou Grant
    b. Murray Slaughter
    c. Ted Baxter
    d. All of the above

20. Who read "The Night Before Christmas" at the Cunninghams's on *Happy Days*'s first Christmas episode?
    a. Howard
    b. Richie
    c. Fonzie
    d. Chuck

ANSWERS

1. d	6. d	11. b	16. c
2. b	7. b	12. c	17. d
3. c	8. a	13. c	18. d
4. a	9. d	14. b	19. d
5. c	10. c	15. c	20. c

JULY 1, 1941

That's the dawn of television—the date the FCC assigned nonexperimental call letters to television stations and permitted commercial advertising. It's the official first day of television. Everything before that was considered experimental. And broadcasting history began, establishing a long list of firsts. The first program. The first newscast. The first commercial.

And, in the age of high-definition and plasma TVs, there are those firsts that get taken for granted. The first color show. The first game show. The first sitcom, medical drama, and soap opera.

There are so many things we've come to love about our favorite shows, but nothing compares to the first time. That's part of the magic of pilot episodes—the first meeting of characters that we'll grow to love. And after the shows have developed their history, we can think back upon some of their signature moments—the firsts. In business, you wouldn't forget your first client.

How about the first customer that walked into Cheers? Or the first one to win *Survivor*? Or the first member of the M*A*S*H 4077 that got to go home?

How many of these famous firsts do you remember?

1. While the first wedding was telecast as an experiment from an Illinois radio station in 1928, when was the first televised proposal (hint: Ahmad Rashad and Phylicia Ayers Allen)?
    a. 1982
    b. 1983
    c. 1984
    d. 1985

2. What was the first science fiction series on television?
    a. *Buck Rogers*
    b. *Captain Video and the Video Rangers*
    c. *Rocky Jones Space Ranger*
    d. *Flash Gordon*

3. Which TV couple was the first to be shown sharing the same bed?
    a. Mike and Carol Brady (*Brady Bunch*)
    b. Darrin and Samantha Stevens (*Bewitched*)
    c. Ricky and Lucy Ricardo (*I Love Lucy*)
    d. Fred and Ethel Mertz (*I Love Lucy*)

4. Which was the first series to show a gay couple in bed together?
    a. *Roseanne*
    b. *thirtysomething*
    c. *Soap*
    d. *Northern Exposure*

5. What was the first TV series that featured a leading woman as a police officer?
    a. *Decoy*
    b. *Police Woman*
    c. *Cagney and Lacey*
    d. *She's the Sheriff*

6. In the *Star Trek* episode where McCoy first said, "He's dead, Jim," who did Spock first use the Vulcan neck pinch on?
   a. Unnamed Klingon
   b. Khan
   c. Harry Mudd
   d. Evil Kirk

7. On the *Cheers*'s episode when Sam's brother Derek asked Diane to go to Paris with him, which other event happened on the show for the first time?
   a. Norm's wife Vera called
   b. Carla mentioned the names of all her children
   c. Sam and Diane kissed
   d. Coach mentioned his daughter

8. When Richie and his friends first form a band on an episode of *Happy Days*, who was mentioned for the first time?
   a. Arnold
   b. Chuck
   c. Potsie
   d. Chachi

9. On the episode of *Seinfeld* where Elaine appeared for the first time, what did George do for the first time?
   a. Referred to himself in the third person
   b. Used the name "Art Vandelay"
   c. Complained about worlds colliding
   d. Went to work for the Yankees

10. Who was the first celebrity Lucy met when the cast of *I Love Lucy* went to Hollywood?
    a. Richard Widmark
    b. John Wayne
    c. William Holden
    d. Harpo Marx

11. What did Janet, Chrissy, and Jack accidentally do to Mr. Furley before they met him for the first time on *Three's Company*?
    a. Rent his apartment
    b. Sell his furniture
    c. Wreck his car
    d. Flood his apartment

12. In order to help Nick with his son David, what job did Monica get when she first became a case worker on *Touched by an Angel*?
    a. Substitute teacher
    b. Guidance Counselor
    c. Nanny
    d. Maid

13. What did Jim do the first time he appeared on *Taxi*?
    a. Took his driver's license test
    b. Performed Latka's wedding ceremony
    c. Wrecked Cab 804
    d. Gave Louie one of his "brownies"

14. Where did Opie get a job on the first color episode of *The Andy Griffith Show*?
    a. Grocery store
    b. Floyd's barber shop
    c. Drug store
    d. Mayberry newspaper

15. Which character made their first appearance on *The Dick Van Dyke Show* when Rob's brother Stacey, who was a sleepwalker, auditioned for *The Alan Brady Show*?
    a. Mel Cooley
    b. Stacey Petrie
    c. Alan Brady
    d. Jerry Helper

16. Who was the first character from *Cheers* to make a guest appearance on *Frasier*?
    a. Sam Malone
    b. Woody Boyd
    c. Lilith Sternin
    d. Cliff Claven

17. On the episode when Deep Throat told Scully and Mulder about a UFO shot down over Iraq on *The X-Files*, who made their first appearance?
    a. Cigarette Smoking Man
    b. Well-Manicured Man
    c. Deep Throat
    d. Lone Gunmen

18. Who was the first guest star on *The Carol Burnett Show*?
    a. Jim Nabors
    b. Sid Caesar
    c. Liza Minelli
    d. Jonathan Winters

19. Who first introduced Johnny Carson on his first night as host of *The Tonight Show*?
    a. Ed McMahon
    b. Skitch Henderson
    c. Groucho Marx
    d. Jerry Lewis

20. Who was the first rock band to appear on *The Simpsons*, performing at the newly christened "Flaming Moes"?
    a. The Who
    b. Aerosmith
    c. U2
    d. Smashing Pumpkins

ANSWERS

1. d	6. d	11. b	16. c
2. b	7. c	12. c	17. d
3. d	8. a	13. b	18. a
4. b	9. b	14. a	19. c
5. a	10. c	15. c	20. b

"WITH ME, AS ALWAYS, IS GARTH"

Second bananas have always been important in television, although they rarely get their due. Of course, that's part of the nature of being the second banana. Still, you can't really imagine *The Tonight Show Starring Johnny Carson* without Ed McMahon. Or *The Honeymooners* without Ed Norton. Or Mork without Mindy.

How much do you remember about these second bananas?

1. What was Buddy Sorrell preparing for the only time he was serious on *The Dick Van Dyke Show*?
   a. His wedding
   b. Gall bladder surgery
   c. His annual employee evaluation
   d. His Bar Mitzvah

2. What real country singer replaced Andy in Jim's band, inviting them to perform with him at the House of Blues, on *According to Jim*?
   a. Kenny Chesney
   b. Brad Paisley
   c. Toby Keith
   d. Tim McGraw

3. When Willie got depressed when he turned forty-five, what activity did *Alf* suggest he do to feel better?
   a. Bungee jumping
   b. Hang gliding
   c. Skydiving
   d. Skiing

4. What celebrity was Vera's sixth cousin, whom she tried to get to endorse Mel's chili on *Alice*?
   a. Jackie Gleason
   b. Art Carney
   c. Telly Savalas
   d. George Burns

5. When Lowell got $20,000 from his trust fund, what did he invest it in on *Wings*?
   a. Lowell Mather's House o' Pancakes
   b. Lowell Mather's House o' Tools
   c. Lowell Mather's House o' Doorknobs
   d. Lowell Mather's House o' Wax

6. What happened to the novel Donald was writing on *That Girl*?
   a. Ann lost it
   b. Ann hated it
   c. Ann sold it to her agent
   d. Ann spilled wine all over it

7. Why was Joe Dominguez forced to rejoin the police force on *Nash Bridges*?
   a. Lost a bet with Nash
   b. Pension dispute
   c. To save his son J. J.
   d. Lost his business in an Internet scam

8. What was Mindy's job on *Mork and Mindy*?
   a. Writer for Boulder newspaper
   b. Writer for Boulder magazine
   c. Clerk at her father's store
   d. Accountant for Mr. Bickley

9. Why did Barney Fife get kicked out of his room on *The Andy Griffith Show*?
   a. He accidently fired his gun in the house
   b. He cooked in his room
   c. His patrol car in the driveway made people think there was trouble there
   d. His snoring disturbed the other boarders

10. When Dick Grayson (Robin's alter ego) went undercover to try and get Susie to lead him into the Bad Pennies, what super villain was he actually after on *Batman*?
    a. Joker
    b. Penguin
    c. Riddler
    d. Catwoman

11. What was Howard Borden's son's name on *The Bob Newhart Show*?
    a. Gordon
    b. Michael
    c. Howie
    d. Bob

12. Who guest-starred as Roger Healey's girlfriend Tina on *I Dream of Jeannie*?
    a. Jaclyn Smith
    b. Kate Jackson
    c. Farrah Fawcett
    d. Cheryl Ladd

13. What did Jack's friend Larry Dallas do for a living on *Three's Company*?
    a. Bartender at Regal Beagle
    b. Car salesman
    c. Lounge singer
    d. Travel agent

14. What did Max name the rose hybrid he created on *Hart to Hart*?
    a. Hart's Love Rose
    b. J. and J. Rose
    c. Jennifer Hart Rose
    d. Double Hart Rose

15. What was Mr. Woodman's first name on *Welcome Back, Kotter*?
    a. Michael
    b. Vincent
    c. Howie
    d. Gordon

16. On the episode when David Addison heard that Maddie was pregnant, what song did Herbert Viola sing on *Moonlighting*?
    a. "Baby Love"
    b. "The Lady Is a Tramp"
    c. "Sexual Healing"
    d. "Wooly Bully"

17. On *The West Wing*, who uncovered the evidence of an affair that led Vice President John Hoynes to tender his resignation?
    a. C. J. Craig
    b. Joc Quincy
    c. Donna Moss
    d. Josh Lyman

18. Who was the first to discover that Kramer's first name was "Cosmo" on *Seinfeld*?
    a. Jerry
    b. Elaine
    c. George
    d. Newman

19. Which of the following "Kookie-isms" (slang phrases spoken by Kookie) meant something was terrific on *77 Sunset Strip*?
    a. Dark seven
    b. Smoggin' the noggin'
    c. King's jive
    d. Ginchiest

20. When Fred hypnotized Barney, and was unable to unhypnotize him, what was Barney left behaving as on *The Flintstones*?
    a. Puppy
    b. Kitten
    c. Chicken
    d. Fred

ANSWERS			
1. d	**6.** a	**11.** c	**16.** c
2. b	**7.** b	**12.** c	**17.** b
3. c	**8.** c	**13.** b	**18.** c
4. b	**9.** b	**14.** c	**19.** d
5. d	**10.** a	**15.** a	**20.** a

WHAT WERE THEY THINKING?

very once in a while, a show appears that is so bad, or so strange, or both, that you can't help wonder what the networks were thinking when they put it on the air. *Manimal?* *Cop Rock?* Three different series based on *Animal House?* It also makes you wonder what shows didn't meet those high standards, and never saw the light of day.

Other times, a program will run a weird storyline, that makes the viewer feel the same thing. *The Harlem Globetrotters on Gilligan's Island?* An all-singing episode of *Buffy the Vampire Slayer?* An entire season of *Dallas* that was a dream?

How much do you remember about these TV mishaps?

1. Who was responsible for *Cop Rock?*
   a. Stephen Bochco
   b. 20th Century Fox Television
   c. ABC
   d. They all share the blame

2. Which was the only *Animal House* series that included actors that appeared in the original movie?
   a. *Delta House*
   b. *Brothers and Sisters*
   c. *Co-ed Fever*
   d. None of the actors were willing to appear in any of them

3. On *Manimal*, while in his human form, what did Jonathan Chase do for a living?
   a. Police detective
   b. Veterinarian
   c. College professor
   d. The show didn't last long enough to establish his career

4. How did Ben Vereen's character get the nickname "Tenspeed" on *Tenspeed and Brownshoe*?
   a. Slang for con man
   b. Slang for motorcycle cop
   c. Slang for racecar driver
   d. Slang for bike messenger

5. When Andrew Dice Clay starred as a TV dad on *Bless This House*, where did his character Burt work?
   a. Nowhere, he was on unemployment
   b. Post office
   c. Bowling alley
   d. Used car dealership

6. Who did the Harlem Globetrotters play basketball against when they appeared on the 1981 *Gilligan's Island* TV movie that nearly spawned a new series?
   a. Russians
   b. Headhunters
   c. Castaways
   d. Robots

7. Who didn't make a crossover guest appearance on the short-lived *Three's Company* spin-off *The Ropers*?
   a. Jack Tripper
   b. Janet Wood
   c. Cindy Snow
   d. Larry Dallas

8. On the quickly cancelled sitcom *Woops!*, how was Mark, the former English teacher, saved during the nuclear holocaust?
   a. He was in a bank vault
   b. He was in a bomb shelter
   c. He was in his Volvo
   d. The show wasn't on long enough to establish that

9. Who joined David Soul (who starred in the Humphrey Bogart role) in the 1983 prequel series *Casablanca*?
   a. Scatman Crothers
   b. Hector Elizondo
   c. Ray Liotta
   d. Can you believe it? They were all in it!

10. After *Happy Days*, where did Joanie and Chachi move for their quickly cancelled series *Joanie Loves Chachi*?
    a. Hollywood
    b. New York
    c. Chicago
    d. They stayed in Milwaukee

11. Where did the majority of *Life with Lucy*, Lucille Ball's short-lived 1986 sitcom, take place?
    a. Her hardware store
    b. Her record store
    c. Her bookstore
    d. Her diner

12. According to *The Bradys*, the hour-long drama that debuted and was cancelled in 1990, what had become of Bobby Brady?
    a. He was paralyzed in an auto accident
    b. He was getting over the death of his wife
    c. He had AIDs
    d. He got fired for having an affair with a coworker

13. Who starred in 1965 as the lawyer David Crabtree who discovered his mother had been reincarnated as a 1928 Porter in *My Mother the Car*?
    a. Jerry Van Dyke
    b. Dick Van Dyke
    c. Dick York
    d. Dick Sargent

14. Who broke into Stalag 13 on the first episode of the World War II POW camp sitcom *Hogan's Heroes*?
    a. Cpl. Lebeau
    b. Cpl. Newkirk
    c. Sgt. Carter
    d. Sgt. Kinchloe

15. Which two members of the original *Star Trek* series made guest appearances on *Homeboys from Outer Space*?
    a. James Doohan and George Takei
    b. William Shatner and Nichelle Nichols
    c. George Takei and Nichelle Nichols
    d. James Doohan and Leonard Nimoy

16. Like *Love Boat* on the rails, *Supertrain* featured guest appearances from what *M*A*S*H* stars in its short run in the spring of 1979?
    a. Loretta Swit
    b. Larry Linville
    c. Jamie Farr
    d. Somehow, they all did!

17. Why didn't Darva Conger want to marry "multimillionaire" Rick Rockwell on *Who Wants to Marry a Multi-Millionaire*?
    a. She was only on the show for the fun of it
    b. She didn't want to have kids and he did
    c. She didn't want to convert to Catholicism
    d. She didn't want to quit her job, and he wanted her to

18. While Matt lived as a high school student even though he was a prince from another planet, who played Walt, his guardian, on *The Powers of Matthew Star*?
    a. Gregory Hines
    b. Louis Gossett Jr.
    c. Bill Cosby
    d. Denzel Washington

19. Which character had the "dream" that encompassed the entire ninth season of *Dallas*?
    a. Pam
    b. Sue Ellen
    c. Angelica
    d. Mandy

20. On *Buffy the Vampire Slayer*, who summoned the demon that caused all the characters to sing?
    a. Dawn
    b. Xander
    c. Willow
    d. Spike

ANSWERS			
1. d	6. d	11. a	16. d
2. a	7. c	12. a	17. a
3. c	8. c	13. a	18. b
4. a	9. d	14. c	19. a
5. b	10. c	15. a	20. b

VERY SPECIAL EPISODES

Many shows have added morals to their stories—simple life lessons from the stars to you. Unfortunately, some shows have gotten a little too preachy, and the effectiveness of this as a tool has waned. Typically, the Very Special Episode is used by sitcoms, where an often amusing cast suddenly turn serious, and remind you about the dangers of drinking and driving, among other things.

How much do you remember about these shows' Very Special Episodes?

1. What did Uncle Bill help Buffy do when she met a very sick girl who might not live much longer, played by the *Brady Bunch's* Eve Plumb, on *Family Affair*?
   a. Throw the sick girl a birthday party, since she might not live until her birthday
   b. Throw the sick girl a Christmas party, since she might not live that long
   c. Donate blood so the girl might live
   d. Take care of the sick girl's kitten, since she might not live much longer

2. Who thought Six was suffering from Bulimia on *Blossom*?
   a. Nick
   b. Anthony
   c. Joey
   d. Blossom

3. What concert did Rerun get caught illegally taping for bootleggers on *What's Happening*?
   a. Elton John
   b. Doobie Brothers
   c. Kool and the Gang
   d. Donna Summer

4. Who was the first person Chachi told he had diabetes on *Happy Days*?
   a. Fonzie
   b. Joanie
   c. Marion
   d. Al

5. Which one of the Sweathogs got hooked on pain pills on *Welcome Back, Kotter*?
   a. Freddie
   b. Vinnie
   c. Horshack
   d. Epstein

6. Who appeared on *Family Ties* as a relative of the Keatons who had a drinking problem?
   a. Courtney Cox
   b. Tom Hanks
   c. Julia Louis-Dreyfus
   d. Timothy Busfield

7. When Niles feared there was something wrong, who was the first person he confided in, before he ended up going to the hospital and having heart bypass surgery on *Frasier*?
   a. Frasier
   b. Martin
   c. Daphne
   d. Roz

8. What event led *The West Wing* to air a stand-alone episode outside of all its storylines?
   a. Terrorist attacks of September 11th
   b. Election problems of 2000
   c. Death of Ronald Reagan
   d. Unexplained blackout of the northeastern United States

9. Who insisted that Murphy get a mammogram, leading to the discovery that she had breast cancer, on *Murphy Brown*?
   a. Frank
   b. Corky
   c. Miles
   d. Kay

10. What was the premise of *Beavis and Butthead*'s "Very Special Episode"?
    a. Beavis's parents were getting divorced
    b. Butthead was getting expelled from school
    c. Beavis's brother got deployed to the Gulf War
    d. The boys found and cared for a wounded bird

11. What future *Friends*'s star taught Carol a valuable lesson about drinking and driving on *Growing Pains*?
    a. David Schwimmer
    b. Matthew Perry
    c. Matt LeBlanc
    d. Courtney Cox

12. Which one of the Huxtable kids got drunk at a party and needed a ride home from an older sibling on *The Cosby Show*?
   a. Denise
   b. Theo
   c. Vanessa
   d. Rudy

13. On *M*A*S*H*, who dealt with their dependence on alcohol, finally deciding they'd come back for a drink when they wanted one, not when they needed one?
   a. Hawkeye Pierce
   b. Trapper John McEntyre
   c. Radar O'Reilly
   d. Henry Blake

14. Who joined Alcoholics Anonymous on *Cagney and Lacey*?
   a. Christine Cagney
   b. Mary Beth Lacey
   c. Harvey Lacey
   d. Manny Espisito

15. Who did Drew help get into rehab after they were discovered doing cocaine on *The Drew Carey Show*?
   a. Lewis
   b. Oswald
   c. Steve
   d. Wick

16. Who started smoking on the first episode of *7th Heaven*?
   a. Matt
   b. Mary
   c. Simon
   d. Lucy

17. Who got caught with cigarettes on *The Brady Bunch*?
    a. Greg
    b. Marcia
    c. Peter
    d. Jan

18. Who had everyone waiting all day for his blood test to see if he had cancer on *Home Improvement*?
    a. Tim
    b. Brad
    c. Randy
    d. Mark

19. On the first episode of *Becker*, what problem does his youngest patient have?
    a. Inoperable tumor
    b. HIV-positive
    c. Diabetes
    d. Hepatitis

20. Who suggested to *Maude* that she have an abortion?
    a. Carol
    b. Walter
    c. Vivian
    d. Arthur

ANSWERS			
1. b	**6.** b	**11.** b	**16.** a
2. d	**7.** d	**12.** c	**17.** a
3. b	**8.** a	**13.** a	**18.** c
4. a	**9.** b	**14.** a	**19.** b
5. a	**10.** d	**15.** d	**20.** a

GUILTY
PLEASURES

Guilty pleasure is a relatively new term for those shows that seemingly have no value, but somehow, we just can't help watching them, anyway. They make you feel better, like good TV should, but at the same time, they make you feel a little guilty. The programs are typically fan favorites, although they don't necessarily perform well in the ratings or with the critics. While it's a recent phenomon, the truth is there have always been shows that have fit this description. *Desperate Housewives* and *Buffy the Vampire Slayer* are recent examples, but the list goes on, including *Star Trek*, *Gilligan's Island*, and *Mr. Ed*.

How much do you remember about these Guilty Pleasures?

1. Which of the following was not an episode of *The Jerry Springer Show*?
   a. I Slept with My Daughter's Man
   b. Three Pigs and a Trailer
   c. Hillbilly Love
   d. Believe it or not, they've all been episodes of Springer!

2. Before *American Idol*, who appeared and went out on a date on *Blind Date*?
   a. Ryan Seacrest
   b. Paula Abdul
   c. Simon Cowell
   d. All three appeared (and Randy, too)!

3. Who did Cartman's father turn out to be on *South Park*?
   a. Chef
   b. Mr. Mackey
   c. Mr. Garrison
   d. Cartman's mother

4. Which category on *COPS* was so popular it was released on DVD?
   a. Shots Fired
   b. Bad Girls
   c. Caught in the Act
   d. All of the above

5. Which topic was not addressed during the first season of *The Man Show*?
   a. Trampoline Auditions
   b. Oprah
   c. Weddings
   d. Underwear

6. What did *V.I.P.* stand for on Pamela Anderson's show of the same name?
   a. Very Important Persons
   b. Val's Important Protection
   c. Valerie Irons Protection
   d. Violet Indigo Protection

7. Where did the cooking contest show *Iron Chef* originally come from?
   a. Italy
   b. China
   c. Japan
   d. France

8. Before hosting *Fear Factor*, what show was Joe Rogan not on?
   a. *NewsRadio*
   b. *The Man Show*
   c. *Blind Date*
   d. He wasn't on any of these shows!

9. After being cancelled by NBC after one season, *Baywatch* resurfaced in syndication with only one female cast member—who?
   a. Pamela Anderson
   b. Gena Lee Nolin
   c. Erika Eleniak
   d. Yasmine Bleeth

10. Which former *Baywatch* star appeared as a reporter on *BattleBots*?
    a. Carmen Electra
    b. Donna D'Errico
    c. Traci Bingham
    d. All three of them did!

11. Though doing well in the ratings, CBS didn't want to be known as a rural network, so they cancelled which successful sitcom in 1971?
    a. *Mayberry RFD*
    b. *Beverly Hillbillies*
    c. *Green Acres*
    d. They pulled the plug on all three!

12. Where did Buffy go to high school on *Buffy the Vampire Slayer*?
    a. Sunnyville
    b. Sunnydale
    c. Riverdale
    d. Rivermont

13. Who died on the final episode of *Angel*?
    a. Spike
    b. Cordelia
    c. Lindsey
    d. Angel

14. Why was John Cage known as "The Biscuit" on *Ally McBeal*?
    a. He was always ready in 10 minutes
    b. Women described him as tasty
    c. His family was part of a successful flour company
    d. It was never revealed

15. What kind of pie did Agent Cooper like to have with his coffee on *Twin Peaks*?
    a. Cherry
    b. Apple
    c. Pecan
    d. Blueberry

16. What's the license plate on the SUV used on *Queer Eye for the Straight Guy*?
    a. QUEER I
    b. QI-5
    c. FAB 5
    d. FABULOUS

17. On *Alias*, who ran the SD-6?
    a. CIA
    b. FBI
    c. Alliance of Twelve
    d. Russian K-Directorate

18. What's the name of Steve Irwin's dog on *The Crocodile Hunter*?
   a. Sue
   b. Sui
   c. Little Steve
   d. Terri

19. Which was the only castaway that didn't have a first and last name on *Gilligan's Island*?
   a. Gilligan
   b. Skipper
   c. Professor
   d. Mary Ann

20. What were the aliens that only Al could see stealing for fuel on *Married . . . with Children*?
   a. Shoes
   b. Socks
   c. Underwear
   d. Beer

ANSWERS			
1. d	**6.** c	**11.** d	**16.** c
2. a	**7.** c	**12.** b	**17.** c
3. d	**8.** c	**13.** c	**18.** b
4. d	**9.** c	**14.** d	**19.** a
5. a	**10.** d	**15.** a	**20.** b

RELOCATION

Many TV shows have begun with a central character entering a new environment. We meet the rest of the cast just as this character meets them. We were introduced to the gang at WJM just as Mary Richards met them at the beginning of *The Mary Tyler Moore Show*. *The Jeffersons* began when George and Weezie moved from next door to the Bunkers to "a deluxe apartment in the sky." And *Northern Exposure* started with Joel finding himself in Alaska.

Other shows have used new locations to try and pump new life into an established series. *Laverne and Shirley* moved to California. The cast of *Coach* headed to a new opportunity in Orlando. And the Ricardos moved out of their New York apartment to a suburb in Connecticut.

How much do you remember about these shows that changed their locations?

1. Why did *Laverne and Shirley* decide to move to California?
   a. They got fired from the brewery
   b. They got a part in a Troy Donahue movie
   c. Frank offered them jobs in his new restaurant in L.A.
   d. They got a job house-sitting a beachfront mansion

2. What was the name of the Orlando team that Hayden left Minnesota for on *Coach*?
   a. Sunspots
   b. Gators
   c. Marlins
   d. Breakers

3. When *Frasier* moves across the country to take a job as a radio psychiatrist, who suggests Martin move in with him?
   a. Maris
   b. Niles
   c. Daphne
   d. Roz

4. Before he wound up in Bel Air, where was the Fresh Prince living?
   a. Washington, D.C.
   b. New York City
   c. Philadelphia
   d. Chicago

5. Where had the Walsh family moved from when they showed up on *Beverly Hills 90210*?
   a. Milwaukee
   b. Minnesota
   c. Cleveland
   d. Nebraska

6. On her way to Hollywood from New Jersey, why did *Alice* stay in Phoenix?
   a. Ran out of money and needed a job
   b. Her car broke down
   c. Tommy liked it there and wanted to stay
   d. Her late husband was from there

7. Where had *Ed* been a lawyer before he moved back home to Stuckeyville?
   a. New York City
   b. Boston
   c. Philadelphia
   d. Chicago

8. Who was the only cast member on *All in the Family* to appear in the episode when *The Jeffersons* packed and moved out of Queens?
   a. Archie
   b. Edith
   c. Gloria
   d. Mike

9. What event brought Syd back to Rhode Island on *Providence*?
   a. Jim and Lynda's anniversary
   b. Jim's heart attack
   c. Lynda's death
   d. Jim's death

10. What did Fred and Ethel decide to do so they could stay in Connecticut with the Ricardos on *I Love Lucy*?
    a. Raise chickens
    b. Sell the apartments in New York and retire
    c. Run a dairy
    d. Manage Ricky's new nightclub

11. Where did Rhoda Morganstern live when she first moved back from Minneapolis to New York on *Rhoda*?
    a. With Brenda
    b. With Ida and Martin
    c. With Joe
    d. She found her own apartment in Brenda's building

12. After moving out of the apartment he shared with Balki and getting married to Jennifer, why did Larry ask Balki to move into his new house on *Perfect Strangers*?
    a. Balki had nowhere to go
    b. Balki was thinking of going back to Mypos
    c. Larry and Jennifer couldn't afford the new house on their own
    d. Larry missed him

13. After he moved from Minneapolis to Los Angeles, who was the only character from *The Mary Tyler Moore Show* that came to visit on *Lou Grant*?
    a. Mary Richards
    b. Ted Baxter
    c. Murray Slaughter
    d. No one from *The Mary Tyler Moore Show* ever appeared on *Lou Grant*

14. In what state was Walnut Grove, where the Ingalls's family settled at the beginning of *The Little House on the Prairie*?
    a. Nebraska
    b. Kansas
    c. Wisconsin
    d. Minnesota

15. Which of the three kids was the first to show up on Bill Davis's doorstep on *Family Affair*?
    a. Buffy
    b. Jody
    c. Cissy
    d. They all arrived together

16. Before he moved to Cicely, where did Joel Fleischman think he was going to be working on *Northern Exposure*?
    a. Nome, Alaska
    b. Anchorage, Alaska
    c. Seattle, Washington
    d. Vancouver, Washington

17. Who convinced Jed to move his family to Beverly Hills after he struck it rich on *The Beverly Hillbillies*?
    a. Jethro Bodine
    b. Pearl Bodine
    c. Milton Drysdale
    d. John Brewster

18. Who sold Oliver Douglas the farm on *Green Acres*?
    a. Mr. Haney
    b. Sam Drucker
    c. Fred Ziffel
    d. Eb Dawson

19. Who didn't make the move from *Saved by the Bell* to *Saved by the Bell: The College Years*?
    a. Zack
    b. Screech
    c. Slater
    d. Jessie

20. What was the name of the moving company that had all of Joey's belongings when he moved from New York to L.A. on *Joey*?
    a. Moving on Up
    b. Movers and Shakers
    c. Earth Moves
    d. Move Over and Over

ANSWERS			
1. a	**6.** b	**11.** b	**16.** b
2. d	**7.** a	**12.** c	**17.** b
3. b	**8.** b	**13.** d	**18.** a
4. c	**9.** c	**14.** d	**19.** d
5. b	**10.** a	**15.** a	**20.** b

CROSSING OVER

BS introduced and perfected this technique in the 1960s—a character from one show would make an appearance on another, as that same character. Characters from *The Beverly Hillbillies*, *Green Acres*, and *Petticoat Junction* were continuously showing up on each others' shows.

In more recent years, this has been used as a way to spin off characters onto their own shows. *Laverne and Shirley* showed up on *Happy Days*, then surfaced on their own show. The same thing happened when Jake Hanson appeared on *Beverly Hills 90210* for a few shows, before kicking off *Melrose Place*.

Other times, the effect has been used as more of a surprise, as when Kramer got a job as a one of *Murphy Brown's* quickly fired secretaries. Or when Phil Drummond and George Jefferson appeared on *Fresh Prince of Bel Air*.

How much do you remember about these cross-over episodes?

1. Which anniversary were Oliver and Lisa Douglas planning on celebrating at *Petticoat Junction*'s Shady Rest Hotel on *Green Acres*?
   a. Fifth
   b. Seventh
   c. Tenth
   d. Twelfth

2. Whose baby did Granny (from *The Beverly Hillbillies*) come to take care of on *Petticoat Junction*?
   a. Bobby Jo's
   b. Betty Jo's
   c. Billie Jo's
   d. Janet Craig's

3. Other than *Homicide: Life on the Street*, where did Richard Belzer's Detective Munch appear?
   a. *Law and Order*
   b. *Law and Order: SVU*
   c. *The X-Files*
   d. All of the above

4. How long had Scotty been missing when the crew of the Enterprise found him on *Star Trek: The Next Generation*?
   a. 25 years
   b. 50 years
   c. 75 years
   d. 100 years

5. Which actor from *The Practice* appeared on *Ally McBeal*?
   a. Dylan McDermott
   b. Lara Flynn Boyle
   c. Austin Tichenor
   d. All of the above

6. Whose murder did *Cannon* help solve on the first episode of *Barnaby Jones*?
   a. Jones's son
   b. Jones's wife
   c. Jones's daughter
   d. Jones's partner

7. When Doug got his driving license suspended on *King of Queens*, which characters from *Everybody Loves Raymond* did he meet?
   a. Ray Barone
   b. Robert Barone
   c. Ray and Robert Barone
   d. Ray, Robert, and Frank Barone

8. What were Jamie and Paul doing on *Mad About You* that led to Paul giving up the apartment he was subletting to *Seinfeld*'s Kramer?
   a. Moving to a bigger place
   b. Writing their wills
   c. Doing their taxes
   d. Gathering things to donate to charity

9. On another episode of *Mad About You*, who did Paul work with from *The Dick Van Dyke Show*?
   a. Rob Petrie
   b. Sally Rogers
   c. Buddy Sorrell
   d. Alan Brady

10. What did Willow (from *Buffy the Vampire Slayer*) travel to L.A. to tell *Angel*?
    a. Cordelia was dead
    b. Buffy was dead
    c. Spike was dead
    d. Spike was back

11. What was the objective of the villain that used female robots and kidnapped Oscar Goldman on *The Bionic Woman* (who was helped by Steve Austin from *The Six Million Dollar Man*)?
    a. Releasing political prisoners
    b. Taking over OSI
    c. Obtaining an experimental weather control machine
    d. Developing a super-race of robots to attack Russia and start World War III

12. Who appeared on *Diagnosis Murder* as Mark Sloane's old friend, who helped defend Jesse when he was falsely accused of murder?
    a. Perry Mason
    b. Ben Matlock
    c. Joyce Davenport
    d. Leland McKenzie

13. What show did Mike Connors reprise his character Joe Mannix on?
    a. *Diagnosis Murder*
    b. *The Fall Guy*
    c. *Here's Lucy*
    d. All of the above

14. On a crossover with characters from *Magnum, P.I.*, who was used as bait to catch a con artist in Hawaii on *Simon and Simon*?
    a. Rick Simon
    b. A. J. Simon
    c. Thomas Magnum
    d. Jonathan Higgins

15. When Thomas Magnum was accused of killing a hitman, whom did he get to help clear him?
    a. Jessica Fletcher from *Murder She Wrote*
    b. Rick and A. J. from *Simon and Simon*
    c. Jim Rockford from *The Rockford Files*
    d. Dave and Maddie from *Moonlighting*

16. On the series finale of *Fresh Prince of Bel Air*, who ended up buying the family's mansion?
    a. Phil Drummond from *Diff'rent Strokes*
    b. J. J. Evans from *Good Times*
    c. George and Louise Jefferson from *The Jeffersons*
    d. Cliff and Claire Huxtable from *The Cosby Show*

17. Who did *ER*'s Dr. Susan Lewis go to New York to try and find, with help from some of the cast of *Third Watch*?
    a. Her sister, Chloe
    b. Her niece, Little Suzie
    c. Her brother-in-law, Joe
    d. Her father, Dan

18. While Jordan Cavanaugh and Woody Hoyt (from *Crossing Jordan*) head to *Las Vegas* to help Ed Deline solve the murder of a high-roller, what singer was trying to convince Delina to allow him to film his next music video there?
    a. Snoop Dogg
    b. P. Diddy
    c. Jay Z
    d. Usher

19. What famous singer hired *Charlie's Angels* to come to *Vega$*, where they got help from Dan Tana to solve a pair of murders?
    a. Frank Sinatra
    b. Sammy Davis Jr.
    c. Dean Martin
    d. Isaac Hayes

20. What led *Seinfeld*'s Kramer to head west, where he ended up getting a part on an episode of *Murphy Brown*?
    a. Jerry asked Kramer to return his key to Jerry's apartment
    b. Jerry asked Elaine to pick up his mail instead of Kramer
    c. His subscription to *TV Guide* ran out
    d. He wanted to go to a California Pizza Kitchen in California

ANSWERS			
1. c	6. a	11. c	16. c
2. b	7. d	12. b	17. b
3. d	8. b	13. d	18. a
4. c	9. d	14. b	19. c
5. d	10. b	15. a	20. a

GOBBLE THE WONDER TURKEY

Thanksgiving is another holiday that turns up on a lot of programs. As with Christmas episodes, you get all the antics of trying to gather the family together, but there's no question of religion, a touchy subject for television even now. In fact, most of the Thanksgiving-themed shows simply deal with the meal (both preparation and aftermath)—a common enough event with which we can all identify, whether you have kids or not, whether you're religious or not.

How much do you remember about these Thanksgiving episodes?

1. Who did the mayor get into a fight with during a live Thanksgiving TV broadcast from City Hall on *Spin City*?
   a. Mike
   b. Paul
   c. Stuart
   d. His father

2. Which character on *Friends* hated Thanksgiving?
   a. Chandler
   b. Phoebe
   c. Rachel
   d. Ross

3. On *That '70s Show*, who did Kelso bring to the Forman's as his Thanksgiving date?
   a. Eric's sister, Laurie
   b. Jackie
   c. Donna
   d. Eric's math teacher

4. What new job did Jackie finally tell her mother she had over Thanksgiving on *Roseanne*?
   a. Construction worker
   b. Police officer
   c. Waitress
   d. Taxi driver

5. Where did the Thanksgiving food fight take place on *Cheers*?
   a. Carla's house
   b. Norm's house
   c. Sam's house
   d. Melville's

6. On *The Simpsons*, why did Bart run away on Thanksgiving, winding up in a homeless story on the news after having dinner at a shelter?
   a. Sent to his room with no supper after he got another "F" on his report card
   b. Sent to his room with no supper after destroying Lisa's centerpiece
   c. Sent to his room after he set the kitchen on fire trying to make real pilgrim food
   d. Sent to his room after letting his dog eat the turkey

7. Who first explained Thanksgiving to Dick on *3rd Rock from the Sun?*
a. Mary
b. Nina
c. Mrs. Dubacek
d. a janitor

8. While Mary and Carlos were planning to go to Puerto Rico, and many of the rest of the family had other plans, who was doing the cooking for the Camdens's holiday dinner on *7th Heaven?*
a. Simon
b. Ruthie
c. Lucy
d. Matt

9. Who swore they thought turkeys could fly on *WKRP in Cincinnati?*
a. Johnny Fever
b. Arthur Carlson
c. Herb Tarlek
d. Les Nessman

10. What did *Will and Grace* encourage Jack to do on Thanksgiving?
a. Meet his son
b. Tell his mother he was gay
c. Tell his mother he's unemployed
d. Get a job

11. What was wrong with the turkeys Mel bought for the orphans on *Alice?*
a. They were stolen
b. They were still alive
c. They were delivered to another restaurant
d. They were sick

12. Who had a childhood fear of Thanksgiving parades on
    Veronica's Closet?
    a. Veronica
    b. Olive
    c. Perry
    d. Leo

13. When Debra cooked Thanksgiving dinner instead of Marie,
    what did she decide to make instead of turkey on *Everybody
    Loves Raymond*?
    a. Fish
    b. Ham
    c. Meatloaf
    d. Chicken cacciatore

14. On *Happy Days*, what did Marion do when everyone was
    watching the football game and ignoring her on Thanksgiving?
    a. Refused to cook dinner
    b. Left and went to her mother's
    c. Left and went to talk to Fonzie
    d. Turned off the TV and told them the story of the first
       Thanksgiving

15. Who was on their way to bowling a perfect game when the
    power went out on Thanksgiving on *According to Jim*?
    a. Jim
    b. Cheryl
    c. Andy
    d. Dana

16. Why didn't Jed want to kill the turkey that had wandered
    over from the Drysdale's on *The Beverly Hillbillies*?
    a. It didn't belong to them
    b. It was Elly May's pet
    c. It kept wanting to shake hands
    d. He didn't want to make more work for Granny

17. When Aunt Clara sent them to the seventeenth-century New England, who got charged with witchcraft on *Bewitched*?
    a. Samantha Stevens
    b. Darrin Stevens
    c. Aunt Clara
    d. Gladys Kravitz

18. Who got a pet turkey on *Married . . . with Children*?
    a. Al
    b. Peg
    c. Kelly
    d. Bud

19. When the Loudons joined Stephanie and her family for Thanksgiving, why did they all leave early on *Newhart*?
    a. Stephanie's parents had thrown away her favorite toy
    b. Stephanie's parents got into a huge fight
    c. Stephanie's parents were offended by something Dick said
    d. It started to snow

20. What bad news did Joel get on Thanksgiving on *Northern Exposure*?
    a. His fiancée was calling off their engagement
    b. He was going to have to work through the holiday
    c. His contract with Cicely was being extended for another year
    d. Maggie was falling for Mike

ANSWERS			
1. d	6. b	11. a	16. c
2. a	7. d	12. c	17. b
3. d	8. c	13. a	18. c
4. b	9. b	14. d	19. b
5. a	10. b	15. a	20. c

SWEEPS

S **weeps is the** ratings period for television. It comes around three times a year—November, February, and May. In the battle for ratings, programs tend to schedule special events, guest appearances, and stunts to attract viewers. We found out who shot J. R. during November sweeps. The final episode of M*A*S*H aired during February sweeps. And Ross and Rachel finally got back together during May sweeps.

How much do you remember about these sweeps stunts?

1. Who helped Scully dig up Mulder's body, to discover that he was infected with the alien virus, but still alive, on *The X-Files*?
   a. Doggett
   b. Skinner
   c. Krycek
   d. The Lone Gunmen

2. Why did Angela fire Tony during the first season of *Who's the Boss*?
   a. She caught him with another woman and was jealous
   b. He accidentally set the kitchen on fire
   c. She and her ex-husband, Mike, got back together
   d. He embarrassed her when she had an important dinner party

3. What athlete did Andrew introduce a boy to help him learn how to fight for his family on *Touched by an Angel*?
   a. Muhammad Ali
   b. George Foreman
   c. Michael Jordan
   d. Hank Aaron

4. On *Step by Step*, when Frank and Carol found out their wedding wasn't official and planned a new one, when they finally got to a ceremony, who was Frank dressed as?
   a. Superman
   b. Ripper the Rabbit
   c. Giggles the Gorilla
   d. Yo-Yo the Clown

5. While he was innocent, who found himself a suspect in the shooting of Peter White on *St. Elsewhere*?
   a. Dr. Westphal
   b. Dr. Craig
   c. Dr. Chandler
   d. Dr. Fiscus

6. Who led the crew of the *Enterprise* to first meet the Borg on *Star Trek: The Next Generation*?
   a. Guinan
   b. Q
   c. Spock
   d. Sarek

7. What happened to Arnie, when he left Nancy on *Roseanne*?
   a. He ran off with a coworker
   b. He confessed that he was gay, and ran off with his boyfriend
   c. He was killed in a car accident
   d. He was abducted by aliens

8. Who made a rare cameo on *Cheers*, after Norm told Cliff that this guest was using Cliff's jokes?
   a. David Letterman
   b. Johnny Carson
   c. Arsenio Hall
   d. Jerry Springer

9. Why was Coach Riley fired on *Boston Public*?
   a. Accused of sexually harassing a student
   b. Dropped a gay student from the football team
   c. Withheld info about Buttle's affair with Lisa
   d. Had an affair with Marilyn

10. Who followed Cory and Topanga on their honeymoon on *Boy Meets World*?
    a. Shawn
    b. Eric
    c. Amy
    d. Feeny

11. Who did Spike tell Buffy had stolen his image on *Buffy the Vampire Slayer*?
    a. Elton John
    b. Flock of Seagulls
    c. Billy Idol
    d. Marilyn Manson

12. Who did Caroline's balloon injure during the Thanksgiving parade on *Caroline in the City*?
    a. Jean Stapleton
    b. Florence Henderson
    c. Robby Benson
    d. Julie Andrews

13. Who discovered Alicia's heart murmur on *Chicago Hope*?
    a. Dr. Keith Wilkes
    b. Dr. Jeffrey Geiger
    c. Dr. Aaron Shutt
    d. Dr. Kate Austin

14. When a tsunami was headed toward Miami, who discovered the bank robbery plot timed to go with the evacuation on *CSI: Miami*?
    a. Delko
    b. Horatio
    c. Alexx
    d. Calleigh

15. What could Drew have taken instead of the Batmobile in the fast food contest he won on *The Drew Carey Show*?
    a. $250,000
    b. $200,000
    c. $100,000
    d. $50,000

16. Which singer got kidnapped while stopped at the Boar's Nest on *The Dukes of Hazzard*?
    a. Kenny Rogers
    b. Dolly Parton
    c. Waylon Jennings
    d. Loretta Lynn

17. Who had Romano just fired before he was killed by the helicopter on *ER*?
    a. Dr. Gregory Pratt
    b. Dr. Michael Gallant
    c. Dr. John Carter
    d. Nurse Samantha Taggert

18. Who played "Accidental" Amy, who returned to *The George Lopez Show* to try and break up Benny and Randy?
    a. Paris Hilton
    b. Sandra Bullock
    c. Reese Witherspoon
    d. Alicia Silverstone

19. On *Hill Street Blues*, who was shot on the courthouse steps just before they could testify against a gangster?
    a. Mick Belker
    b. Joyce Davenport
    c. Frank Furillo
    d. Henry Goldblume

20. What put Finch's dad, played by Brian Dennehy, in the hospital on *Just Shoot Me*?
    a. Night of drinking with Jack
    b. Night of bar-hopping with Elliott
    c. Night of all-you-can-eat ribs with Jack and Elliott
    d. Night of passion with Nina

ANSWERS			
1. b	6. b	11. c	16. d
2. c	7. d	12. b	17. a
3. a	8. b	13. a	18. b
4. d	9. c	14. b	19. c
5. a	10. b	15. b	20. d

"MISS HATHAWAY, WILL YOU COME IN HERE?"

Many shows allowed us to easily identify with the main characters by giving them an annoying boss. Whose boss hasn't driven them crazy at one time or another? We probably didn't have bosses as greedy as *The Beverly Hillbillies*'s Milton Drysdale or as selfish as Drew Carey's Mr. Wick, but we certainly recognized some of the behavior.

How much do you remember about these TV bosses?

1. On *Taxi*, while Louie was the dispatcher at Sunshine Cab, who was the unseen big boss upstairs?
   a. Mr. DePalmer
   b. Mr. Walters
   c. Mr. MacKenzie
   d. Mr. Phillips

2. When Bud Harper became Tim's new boss on *Home Improvement*, what change did he want to make to *Tool Time*?
   a. More sponsors that would attract female viewers
   b. Change the show's time slot to early Saturday morning
   c. Replace Al
   d. Replace Debbie

3. Who was Lucy's boss at the Unique Employment Agency on *Here's Lucy*?
   a. Mr. Mooney
   b. Uncle Harry
   c. Carter Brothers
   d. Craig Carter

4. What did Ralph's boss, J. J. Marshall (the president of Gotham Bus Company) really mean when he told Ralph to turn in his uniform on *The Honeymooners*?
   a. Ralph was fired
   b. Drivers were getting new uniforms
   c. Drivers were going to have to provide their own uniforms from now on
   d. Ralph was getting promoted

5. Who was Fred's boss at the Quarry on *The Flintstones*?
   a. Mr. Slate
   b. Mr. Spacely
   c. Mr. Cogswell
   d. Mr. Burns

6. Who was J. D.'s boss, the chief of staff, on *Scrubs*?
   a. Bob Kelso
   b. Elliott Reid
   c. Perry Cox
   d. Christopher Turk

7. Who was the first person Donald Trump fired on the first episode of *The Apprentice*?
   a. Tammy Lee
   b. David Gould
   c. Andy Litinsky
   d. No one was fired on the first episode

8. What was the name of Mel's diner on *Alice*?
   a. Mel's Diner
   b. Mel's Taste of Phoenix
   c. Mel's Chili
   d. Mel's Place

9. While Miles ran *F.Y.I.*, who was Murphy's boss, the president of the network, on *Murphy Brown*?
   a. Miles Silverberg
   b. Jim Dial
   c. Miller Redfield
   d. Stan Lansing

10. Which of Elaine's bosses had her buying socks on *Seinfeld*?
    a. Mr. Lippman
    b. Mr. Pitt
    c. J. Peterman
    d. Jack Klompus

11. What was the name of the unseen principal on *Welcome Back, Kotter*?
    a. Lazarus
    b. Caruso
    c. Bordon
    d. Ludlow

12. On *Car 54 Where Are You?*, what did Toody accidentally teach
    the pet parrot of his boss, Capt. Block, to say?
    a. "You're under arrest"
    b. "I hate this job"
    c. "I hate Capt. Block"
    d. "Capt. Block is dumb"

13. What did Hank discover about his boss, Bud Strickland, that
    made him question his devotion to his job on *King of the Hill*?
    a. He had an electric stove
    b. He had a charcoal grill
    c. He was a vegetarian
    d. He was a Redskins' fan

14. Who was Michael's boss, who sent him on his various mis-
    sions, on *Knight Rider*?
    a. RC3
    b. Bonnie Barstow
    c. April Curtis
    d. Devon Miles

15. Who was Napoleon Solo and Illya Kuryakin's boss, the head
    of the agency, on *The Man From U.N.C.L.E.*?
    a. Tracey Alexander
    b. Christopher Larson
    c. Alexander Waverly
    d. Maximillian Harmon

16. Who got kidnapped and offered as an exchange for Captain
    Greer on *The Mod Squad*?
    a. Pete
    b. Linc
    c. Julie
    d. Adam

17. What political office did station manager Arthur Carlson run for on *WKRP in Cincinnati*?
    a. Mayor
    b. City Council
    c. Governor
    d. Congressman

18. When Rebecca took over *Cheers*, what did Norm do to try and pay off his tab?
    a. He did the bar's taxes
    b. He painted her office
    c. He babysat her cousin's kids
    d. He got her a date with Evan

19. Who accidentally announced, on national television, that Rob's boss, Alan Brady, was bald on *The Dick Van Dyke Show*?
    a. Sally
    b. Buddy
    c. Laura
    d. Mel

20. What did Homer's boss, Mr. Burns, do to the town of Springfield that led to his getting shot on *The Simpsons*?
    a. Stole the oil out from under the school
    b. Blocked out the sun
    c. Forgot Homer's name
    d. All of the above

ANSWERS			
1. c	6. a	11. a	16. c
2. c	7. b	12. c	17. b
3. b	8. a	13. a	18. b
4. d	9. d	14. d	19. c
5. a	10. a	15. c	20. d

CHESTER, FESTUS, AND DOC

Westerns were another genre that made their way over to TV from radio. *The Lone Ranger* led the way, followed years later by *Gunsmoke*, which would go on to become one of the longest running television shows ever. While its popularity has waxed and waned over the years, Westerns have remained a staple, from the singing cowboy Gene Autry to its incarnation in the twenty-first century on HBO, *Deadwood*.

How much do you remember about these TV Westerns?

1. When Miss Kitty owned half the Long Branch, who owned the other half on *Gunsmoke*?
   a. Matt Dillon
   b. Bill Pence
   c. Wayne Russell
   d. Newly O'Brien

2. Which state was the setting for *Bonanza*?
   a. Kansas
   b. Colorado
   c. California
   d. Nevada

3. On *The Big Valley*, where was Jarrod Barkley's other law office, the first being in Stockton?
   a. Los Angeles
   b. San Francisco
   c. Denver
   d. Sunnydale

4. Who did James West and Artemus Gordon work for on *Wild Wild West*?
   a. Secret Service
   b. FBI
   c. CIA
   d. U.S. Army

5. Whose medical report got mixed up with Agarn's, making him think he was dying, on *F Troop*?
   a. Bill Colton
   b. Bob Colton
   c. Pete the Bartender
   d. His horse

6. What criminal from the future killed Brisco County Sr., Brisco's father, on *The Adventures of Brisco County Jr.*?
   a. John Bly
   b. Pete Hutter
   c. Professor Wickwire
   d. Socrates Poole

7. What happened to Matthew, Colleen, and Brian's mother, leaving Mike to raise them, on *Dr. Quinn Medicine Woman?*
   a. Died of pneumonia
   b. Shot accidently during a robbery
   c. Died of a rattlesnake bite
   d. Trampled in a stampede

8. Who played Beau "Pappy" Maverick, Bart, and Brett's father (not the character played later by Roger Moore) on *Maverick?*
   a. Robert Colbert
   b. James Garner
   c. Jack Kelly
   d. Peter Breck

9. What was a common trait, even joked about in *Time* magazine as being part of Clint Walker's contract, found in most episodes of *Cheyenne?*
   a. Cheyenne appeared shirtless
   b. Cheyenne was kissed while in chains
   c. Cheyenne was beaten with a whip
   d. Cheyenne was doused with water

10. What was the name of Roy's wonder dog on *The Roy Rogers Show?*
    a. Bullet
    b. Pat
    c. Nellybelle
    d. Dusty

11. Who was Gene's sidekick, while Pat was recovering from an accident, on *The Gene Autry Show?*
    a. Tiny
    b. Sagebrush
    c. Chill Wills
    d. All three of them!

12. While he usually received cash as his fee, when Paladin's tailor was killed in a gold mine, what did he get for his services on *Have Gun, Will Travel*?
    a. His weight in gold
    b. Deed to the gold mine
    c. A golden gun
    d. Two new suits a year for life

13. Who was the trail boss on *Rawhide* before Clint Eastwood's Rowdy Yates was promoted (in the last season)?
    a. Gil Favor
    b. G. W. Wishbone
    c. Bill Rudd
    d. Clay Forrester

14. What was the name of the cook on *Wagon Train*, the only character besides Bill Hawks, who appeared in all eight seasons?
    a. Flint McCullough
    b. Duke Shannon
    c. Charlie Wooster
    d. G. W. Wishbone

15. Before pulling up stakes and moving to the San Fernando Valley, where did *The Real McCoys* live?
    a. West Virginia
    b. Arkansas
    c. Oklahoma
    d. Hooterville

16. Why was Caine pursued by Chinese Imperial agents while he was searching the West for his long-lost brother on *Kung Fu*?
    a. He was accused of stealing valuable jewels from the Chinese Royal Family
    b. He was accused of leaking information to enemies of the Chinese Royal Family
    c. He had an affair with a member of the Chinese Royal Family
    d. He had killed a member of the Chinese Royal Family

17. How were Hannibal Heyes and Kid Curry, the real names of the outlaws on *Alias Smith and Jones*, related?
    a. Brothers
    b. Cousins
    c. Stepbrothers
    d. They weren't related

18. What was the name of the family that owned the ranch named High Chaparral on the series of the same name?
    a. Butler
    b. Cannon
    c. Reno
    d. Montoya

19. What was the name of the marshal who often needed the help of Lucas McCain on *The Rifleman*?
    a. Nels Svenson
    b. Angus Evans
    c. Jay Burrage
    d. Micah Torrence

20. At the end of the first season, who was named the sheriff of *Deadwood*?
    a. Wild Bill Hickock
    b. Seth Bullock
    c. Al Swearengen
    d. Calamity Jane

And The Emmy
Goes To . . .

The Emmy Awards are given to reward excellence in all aspects of television. The statues have been handed out since 1949, though the categories have changed over the years. In fact, there were only half a dozen awards given out in 1949. That number increased by nearly one hundred in 2004.

As with the Oscars, the winners weren't always the most popular choices. On the other hand, Emmy nominations and, more importantly, Emmy wins, kept several shows from being cancelled.

How much do you remember about these Emmy-winning TV shows?

1. What sitcom has won the most Emmy awards?
    a. *The Mary Tyler Moore Show*
    b. *Cheers*
    c. *Frasier*
    d. *All in the Family*

2. Which actor won an Emmy for both comedy and drama series?
   a. Jack Klugman
   b. Carroll O'Connor
   c. Robert Young
   d. All three (actually they are the only three with that distinction)

3. Who was the only actor to win Emmy awards for acting, directing and writing (though not in the same year)?
   a. Alan Alda
   b. Carroll O'Connor
   c. Carol Burnett
   d. Mary Tyler Moore

4. What TV drama has the most Emmy nominations?
   a. *Hill Street Blues*
   b. *ER*
   c. *L.A. Law*
   d. *West Wing*

5. What TV drama has won the most Emmy awards?
   a. *Hill Street Blues*
   b. *ER*
   c. *L.A. Law*
   d. *West Wing*

6. Which was the first "nonbroadcast" show to win an Emmy?
   a. *The Sopranos*
   b. *Six Feet Under*
   c. *Sex and the City*
   d. *Queer as Folk*

7. While *The Carol Burnett Show* won a total of twenty-five Emmy awards, which cast member won the most?
   a. Tim Conway
   b. Harvey Korman
   c. Vicki Lawrence
   d. Lyle Waggoner

8. On *The Mary Tyler Moore Show*, who won as many total Emmys during the series as Mary Tyler Moore did (7)?
   a. Ed Asner
   b. Ted Knight
   c. Valerie Harper
   d. Betty White

9. Which comedy won the most Emmys as Outstanding Comedy Series?
   a. *Dick Van Dyke Show*
   b. *Cheers*
   c. *All in the Family*
   d. *Frasier*

10. On an Emmy-winning episode of *The West Wing* from the first season, who was Toby trying to arrange a funeral for?
    a. His first college roommate
    b. Inspirational college professor
    c. Homeless veteran
    d. Staff member he'd fired the week before

11. Who got shot in the first episode of *Hill Street Blues*, which won Emmys for writing and directing?
    a. Washington and LaRue
    b. Hill and Renko
    c. Bates and Coffey
    d. Schnitz and Garibaldi

12. Where did Tony Soprano run into a former associate who was now in the witness protection program in an episode of *The Sopranos* that won an Emmy for writing?
    a. While on vacation in Aspen
    b. While taking Meadow on a college tour
    c. While fishing in Maine
    d. While checking out nursing homes for Livia

13. On the first episode of *Arrested Development*, which won Emmys for writing and directing, what did George-Michael answer when his father, Michael Bluth, asked him what the most important thing was?
    a. Family
    b. Knowledge
    c. Money
    d. Breakfast

14. On *Six Feet Under*, who came to their sister Sarah's aid when she went through withdrawal (the guest role of Sarah earned Patricia Clarkson an Emmy)?
    a. Ruth
    b. Claire
    c. David
    d. Nate

15. When Marie accused Debra of not returning a canister on *Everybody Loves Raymond*, who did it turn out actually had it, on an episode that won Patricia Heaton an Emmy?
    a. Ray had it on his desk, filled with pens
    b. Frank was keeping tools in it
    c. Robert was keeping change in it
    d. Debra had it all along

16. Where did Elaine meet John F. Kennedy Jr., leading to her losing "The Contest," an episode that won Emmys for *Seinfeld*?
    a. Waiting in line for a movie
    b. Waiting in line for a table at a restaurant
    c. At her exercise class
    d. At the offices of Pendant Publishing

17. How long did Archie give Edith to have her "change" on an episode of *All in the Family*, which won an Emmy for writing?
    a. An hour
    b. Ten minutes
    c. Five minutes
    d. Thirty seconds

18. What wrong conclusion did Ricky and Fred leap to while Lucy and Ethel incorrectly thought the two men were being drafted into the army on *I Love Lucy*, on an early episode that helped the show win the Best Comedy Emmy?
    a. The girls were pregnant
    b. One of the girls was having an affair
    c. One of the girls was dying
    d. The girls were mad at them

19. For which show did Bill Cosby win three of his four Emmy awards?
    a. *The Cosby Show*
    b. *Cosby*
    c. *The Cosby Mysteries*
    d. *I Spy*

20. What was the only Western to have won the Emmy for Outstanding Drama Series?

 a. *The Lone Ranger*
 b. *Have Gun, Will Travel*
 c. *Gunsmoke*
 d. *Maverick*

ANSWERS			
1. c	**6.** c	**11.** b	**16.** c
2. d	**7.** b	**12.** b	**17.** d
3. a	**8.** a	**13.** d	**18.** a
4. b	**9.** d	**14.** a	**19.** d
5. a	**10.** c	**15.** d	**20.** c

EMMY LOSERS

A **lmost as interesting** as the winners are the Emmy losers. And they are certainly more surprising. Some of the most popular programs and stars have never won. How much do you remember about these Emmy losers?

1. In 2000, when *The West Wing* won nine Emmys, which cast member wasn't even nominated?
   a. Martin Sheen
   b. Rob Lowe
   c. Stockard Channing
   d. John Spencer

2. While he never won an Emmy, what was the show that gave Andy Griffith his only nomination?
   a. *Andy Griffith Show*
   b. *Murder In Texas*
   c. *Salvage One*
   d. *Matlock*

3. While *The Beverly Hillbillies* never won a single Emmy, which one of the stars was the only one ever nominated?
   a. Buddy Ebsen
   b. Max Baer
   c. Donna Douglas
   d. Irene Ryan

4. Who was the only cast member from *Star Trek* to be nominated for an Emmy, while the show and its cast never actually won any?
   a. William Shatner
   b. Leonard Nimoy
   c. James Doohan
   d. DeForest Kelley

5. Who didn't win an Emmy (as an actor, writer, director, or producer) on *Seinfeld*?
   a. Jerry Seinfeld
   b. Jason Alexander
   c. Julia Louis-Dreyfus
   d. Michael Richards

6. While *Happy Days* never won an acting Emmy, who never even got nominated?
   a. Ron Howard
   b. Henry Winkler
   c. Tom Bosley
   d. Marion Ross

7. Which star of *M*A*S*H* never won an Emmy?
   a. Alan Alda
   b. Loretta Swit
   c. Jamie Farr
   d. Gary Burghoff

8. While Art Carney was the only one of *The Honeymooners* to win an Emmy, which of the others was never nominated?
   a. Audrey Meadows
   b. Joyce Randolph
   c. Jackie Gleason
   d. None of them were ever nominated

9. Which show garnered the most nomination without winning a single Emmy award?
   a. *Dynasty*
   b. *The Larry Sanders Show*
   c. *Northern Exposure*
   d. *The Sopranos*

10. While it did win lighting and photography Emmys, *Home Improvement* didn't win any acting Emmys and only one of the following even got nominated more than once. Which one?
    a. Tim Allen
    b. Patricia Richardson
    c. Richard Karn
    d. Jonathan Taylor Thomas

11. Who has the most acting Emmy nominations without a single win?
    a. Andy Griffith
    b. Roseanne
    c. Angela Lansbury
    d. John Goodman

12. Which of Lucille Ball's costars was never nominated for an Emmy?
    a. Vivian Vance
    b. Desi Arnaz
    c. Gale Gordon
    d. None of them were ever nominated

13. Which show did Tony Danza's only Emmy nomination come from?
    a. *Taxi*
    b. *Who's the Boss?*
    c. *Family Law*
    d. *The Practice*

14. While *ER* is one of the most honored shows ever, which of the following stars has been nominated the most times (none have won)?
    a. George Clooney
    b. Anthony Edwards
    c. Eriq La Salle
    d. Noah Wyle

15. Which late night host never won an Emmy?
    a. Jay Leno
    b. David Letterman
    c. Johnny Carson
    d. Jack Paar

16. Which one of the cast members of *Friends* was never nominated for an Emmy?
    a. Courtney Cox
    b. Matt LeBlanc
    c. Matthew Perry
    d. David Schwimmer

17. While Barbara Bel Geddes was the only one on *Dallas* to win an acting Emmy, who had the most nominations?
    a. Patrick Duffy
    b. Linda Gray
    c. Larry Hagman
    d. Victoria Principal

18. Guest performers were nominated, and won, Emmys on *The Cosby Show*, but which cast member never got a nomination?
   a. Bill Cosby
   b. Phylicia Rashad
   c. Lisa Bonet
   d. Malcolm-Jamal Warner

19. While none of these shows won a single Emmy, which was nominated the most times?
   a. *Baywatch*
   b. *South Park*
   c. *I Dream of Jeannie*
   d. *Laverne and Shirley*

20. While she has yet to win an Emmy, which show was Heather Locklear nominated for?
   a. *Spin City*
   b. *Melrose Place*
   c. *T. J. Hooker*
   d. She has yet to be nominated

ANSWERS			
1. b	**6.** a	**11.** c	**16.** a
2. b	**7.** c	**12.** b	**17.** c
3. d	**8.** b	**13.** d	**18.** a
4. b	**9.** a	**14.** d	**19.** b
5. b	**10.** b	**15.** d	**20.** d

EVERYTHING'S RELATIVE

Sometimes, as a gimmick, television shows would introduce a new family member. Usually, these were guest stars and it was little more than a stunt for ratings. Occasionally, the character recurred and actually moved the story along. *The Beverly Hillbillies* had Cousin Pearl. Jerry Seinfeld had Uncle Leo. And when John Ritter died, we met several relatives on *8 Simple Rules*.

Some shows just used relatives as punchlines. Most episodes of *Welcome Back, Kotter* began with a story about one of Kotter's aunts or uncles. And *The Addams Family* had a slew of creepy and kooky relatives for any occasion.

How much do you remember about these extended TV family relations?

1. What did Jerry's Uncle Leo find in the garbage that Jerry had just thrown out on *Seinfeld*?
   a. Astronaut pen from Jack Klompus
   b. Watch from his parents
   c. Cashmere sweater with a red dot
   d. Uma Thurman's phone number

2. Which of Samantha's relatives switched her voice with Darrin's on *Bewitched*?
    a. Aunt Clara
    b. Uncle Arthur
    c. Uncle Henry
    d. Cousin Edgar

3. Which *Hee Haw* cast member appeared as one of *The Beverly Hillbillies's* cousins, who came looking to make a record deal?
    a. Roy Clark
    b. Buck Owens
    c. Minnie Pearl
    d. Misty Rowe

4. Who did Tim hire to rebuild the *Tool Time* set on *Home Improvement*?
    a. His brother Jeff
    b. His brother Marty
    c. His cousin Barry
    d. His cousin Alex

5. What did George's cousin Dusty ask him for on *The Jeffersons*?
    a. A job
    b. Money
    c. A place to live
    d. A kidney

6. Whose aunt, voiced by Meryl Streep, lived in Louisiana and allowed her house to be a stop on the guys' trip to the Superdome on *King of the Hill*?
    a. Hank's
    b. Dale's
    c. Bill's
    d. Boomhauer's

7. What was Paul's Uncle Phil (Mel Brooks) on trial for on *Mad About You*?
   a. Shoplifting a ham
   b. Changing prices at a department store
   c. Computer fraud
   d. Coupon fraud

8. What charge did Fran's Uncle Mannie, played by Milton Berle, defend her from on *The Nanny*?
   a. Driving without a chauffeur's license
   b. Having a party without the required licenses
   c. Working as a nanny without the required licenses
   d. Buying drugs from an undercover cop (all a misunderstanding)

9. Who turned out to be Harry' real father on *Night Court*?
   a. Phil Sanders
   b. Buddy Ryan
   c. Mel Torme
   d. Jack Griffin

10. When Chris got his half-brother Bernard to help settle a 150-year-old dispute between two Cicely families, what did Bernard confess that he'd never done on *Northern Exposure*?
    a. Drugs
    b. Drank
    c. Fought
    d. Listened to the radio

11. What did Felix's brother Floyd try to convince him to do on *The Odd Couple*?
    a. Invest in his business
    b. Set him up with Myrna
    c. Move away from New York
    d. Get Murray to fix his ticket

12. Who told Ray to his horror that he was just like his cousin Gerard on *Everybody Loves Raymond*?
    a. Debra
    b. Robert
    c. Frank
    d. Marie

13. What did Roger Phillips, Marion's nephew, do when he first came to Milwaukee on *Happy Days*?
    a. Crashed into Arnold's restaurant
    b. Crashed into Howard's car
    c. Crashed into Cunningham Hardware
    d. Crashed into Fonzie's motorcycle

14. Where did Laverne's Italian cousin Antonio (played by Ed Marinaro) finally decide to get a job on *Laverne and Shirley*?
    a. Pizza bowl
    b. The zoo
    c. Shotz Brewery
    d. Carmine's dance studio

15. What did Jake, the Salinger kids' grandfather, help Bailey decide to do with his college money on *Party of Five*?
    a. Give it to Julia so she could go to college
    b. Use it to save Salinger's, the family restaurant
    c. Give it to Charlie to pay his medical bills
    d. Give it to Jake to pay for his surgery

16. Which is the first Addam's relative, other than the series regulars, to make an appearance on *The Addams Family*?
    a. Cousin Itt
    b. Cousin Melancholia
    c. Cousin Cackle
    d. Uncle Atlas

17. When Tony's Italian relatives visited on *Who's the Boss*, his Uncle Aldo gave him part of the family winery, while Tony's cousin Maurizio wanted to do what?
    a. Move to New York and open a restaurant
    b. Try out for the Yankees
    c. Marry Angela
    d. Learn to cook to impress his girlfriend

18. Who started dating Tony's sister, Monica, on *Taxi*?
    a. Jim
    b. Alex
    c. Louie
    d. Latka

19. How was Cousin Oliver, whose parents were going away to Africa for the summer, related to the Brady family on *The Brady Bunch*?
    a. Mike's nephew
    b. Carol's nephew
    c. Not a blood relative, but the son of Mike's business partner
    d. His relationship was never established

20. While the actors were involved in a dispute with the studio, where did Bo and Luke supposedly go when their cousins Coy and Vance came to town on *The Dukes of Hazzard*?
    a. In search of their parents
    b. Driving Kenny Rogers's tour bus
    c. Racing on the NASCAR circuit
    d. Their disappearance was never officially addressed

ANSWERS			
1. b	6. c	11. c	16. b
2. b	7. d	12. a	17. c
3. a	8. b	13. d	18. a
4. b	9. b	14. b	19. b
5. d	10. c	15. b	20. c

GUEST STARS APPEARING AS THEMSELVES

Stars have been making special appearances since the earliest days of television, usually as a rarely seen relative or to offer comic relief. More memorable, however, has been when the celebrities appeared as themselves. One of the most popular episodes of *All in the Family* was when Sammy Davis Jr. showed up at the Bunkers. And who can forget Marcia finally getting to meet Davy Jones on *The Brady Bunch*? Or when George Costanza asked out Marisa Tomei on *Seinfeld*?

How much do you remember about these celebrity appearances?

1. Why was it so important for Marcia to get in touch with Davy Jones on *The Brady Bunch*?
   a. She needed to replace a friend's autographed picture she accidently ruined
   b. She'd promised he'd perform at the prom
   c. He was the only member of The Monkees she hadn't met
   d. She'd heard he was leaving the country for a two-year tour

2. Who did *Dynasty* cast members run into at Denver's Carousel Ball?
   a. Gerald Ford
   b. Betty Ford
   c. Henry Kissinger
   d. All of the above

3. Who did Lucy accidentally hit in the face with a pie when she went to the Brown Derby on *I Love Lucy*?
   a. Richard Widmark
   b. John Wayne
   c. William Holden
   d. Bob Hope

4. Who showed up on *The Bernie Mac Show* to help Jordan deal with a school bully?
   a. Michael Jordan
   b. George Foreman
   c. Sugar Ray Leonard
   d. The Rock

5. On *Cheers*, who claimed to have gotten a part on a *Spenser for Hire* episode, prompting an appearance by Robert Urich?
   a. Sam
   b. Woody
   c. Cliff
   d. Rebecca

6. What singer brings their car into Ed Brown's garage on *Chico and the Man*?
   a. Tony Orlando
   b. Jose Feliciano
   c. John Denver
   d. Sammy Davis Jr.

7. Which member of *The Osbournes* appeared on several episodes of *Dawson's Creek*?
   a. Jack
   b. Kelly
   c. Sharon
   d. Ozzie

8. Who joined Colt's posse to track down diamond smugglers on *The Fall Guy*?
   a. Gene Autry
   b. Roy Rogers
   c. Clayton Moore
   d. James Arness

9. What was the first sitcom Donald Trump appeared on as himself?
   a. *Fresh Prince of Bel Air*
   b. *The Drew Carey Show*
   c. *Spin City*
   d. *The Nanny*

10. Whose touring baseball team does Bud try to get to come to Springfield on *Father Knows Best*?
   a. Casey Stengel
   b. Duke Snider
   c. Bobby Thompson
   d. Willie Mays

11. What baseball player, who turned up on the show, did Big Jimmy claim to have coached on *Yes, Dear*?
   a. Johnny Bench
   b. Ernie Banks
   c. Frank Robinson
   d. All of the above

12. Who appeared on *Wings* to announce that Roy was in trouble when he (Roy) demanded to get his picture taken with the president?
    a. Nancy Reagan
    b. Barbara Bush
    c. Maury Povich
    d. Edwin Newman

13. Who did Ross meet at Central Perk, making him remake his list of celebrities he could sleep with on *Friends*?
    a. Julia Roberts
    b. Brooke Shields
    c. Isabella Rossellini
    d. Cher

14. Who did Paul see in the virtual reality machine he invested in on *Mad About You*?
    a. Jill Goodacre
    b. Christie Brinkley
    c. Farrah Fawcett
    d. Heather Locklear

15. Why did Sammy Davis Jr. show up at the Bunkers's house on *All in the Family*?
    a. Mike found his briefcase at the library
    b. Archie found his briefcase in his cab
    c. Gloria found his briefcase on the subway
    d. Edith found his briefcase in front of the supermarket

16. Who talked Larry into taking part in the celebrity auction on *Curb Your Enthusiasm*?
    a. Richard Lewis
    b. Rob Reiner
    c. Ed Asner
    d. Ted Danson

17. Which is the only sitcom to feature a guest appearance by Groucho Marx?
    a. *I Love Lucy*
    b. *I Dream of Jeannie*
    c. *The Beverly Hillbillies*
    d. *Make Room for Daddy*

18. On which sitcom did *Jeopardy* host Alex Trebek make his first appearance as himself?
    a. *Cheers*
    b. *Mama's Family*
    c. *Golden Girls*
    d. *Ellen*

19. For whose surprise roast did Walter Cronkite appear on *Murphy Brown*?
    a. Jim Dial's
    b. Murphy Brown's
    c. Frank Fontana's
    d. Stan Lansing's

20. On which TV series did Ed McMahon make his first guest appearance as himself?
    a. *ChiPs*
    b. *Full House*
    c. *Alf*
    d. *Here's Lucy*

ANSWERS			
1. b	6. d	11. d	16. b
2. d	7. a	12. d	17. b
3. c	8. b	13. c	18. b
4. c	9. a	14. b	19. a
5. b	10. b	15. b	20. d

MUSICAL GUESTS IN NONMUSICAL APPEARANCES

ounds like a category from an awards show, doesn't it? So many singers and musicians have tried their hands at acting, they really deserve their own category. This isn't about those that showed up on a popular show to play their latest hit. It's for those who, successfully or not, showed up on our favorite shows in a serious attempt at acting.

How much do you remember about these singers in non-singing roles?

1. After *The Monkees*, what show did Mickey Dolenz first appear on?
   a. *My Three Sons*
   b. *Adam-12*
   c. *Cannon*
   d. *Mike Hammer*

2. On *McCloud*, who guest-starred as Colorado's Deputy Cobb in an episode where McCloud tracked modern-day cattle rustlers?
   a. Dean Martin
   b. John Denver
   c. Tony Orlando
   d. Charlie Daniels

3. While he appeared on all of these shows, which one gave Eagle Glenn Frey his start as an actor?
   a. *Arli$$*
   b. *Wiseguy*
   c. *Nash Bridges*
   d. *Miami Vice*

4. When Josh Groban appeared on *Ally McBeal*, why did he hire Cage and Fish?
   a. To sue a judge for not letting him compete in a singing contest
   b. To sue his parents because he doesn't want to go to college
   c. To sue a girl for not going to the prom with him
   d. To sue a teacher for a poor grade on an oral exam

5. Before he was married to Grace on *Will and Grace*, whose cousin did Harry Connick Jr. play on *Cheers*?
   a. Sam's
   b. Rebecca's
   c. Woody's
   d. Norm's

6. Who did Madonna share an apartment with on *Will and Grace*?
   a. Jack
   b. Karen
   c. Grace
   d. Will

7. While he started his acting career much earlier, which Rat Packer guest-starred when *Charlie's Angels* went to Las Vegas?
   a. Frank Sinatra
   b. Dean Martin
   c. Sammy Davis Jr.
   d. Joey Bishop

8. What purpose did Lyle Lovett's character Lenny serve on *Mad About You*?
   a. He was Murray's original owner
   b. He performed Paul and Jamie's wedding service
   c. He was Mabel's babysitter
   d. He introduced Paul to Jamie

9. When Faith Hill appeared on *Promised Land*, which former Waltons's star also appeared as a drug-impaired driver?
   a. Richard Thomas
   b. Michael Learned
   c. David W. Harper
   d. Judy Norton

10. Which former boy-band member did Phoebe have feelings for on *Charmed*?
    a. Justin Timberlake
    b. Nick Lachey
    c. Nick Carter
    d. Lance Bass

11. Which former boy-band member was hired by Paul to teach Bridget how to play drums on *8 Simple Rules*?
    a. Justin Timberlake
    b. Nick Lachey
    c. Nick Carter
    d. Lance Bass

12. What future singer had recurring roles on *Good Times* and *Diff'rent Strokes*?
    a. Janet Jackson
    b. Mariah Carey
    c. Irene Cara
    d. Deniece Williams

13. On which series did Vanessa Williams appear as a police officer?
    a. *Miami Vice*
    b. *T. J. Hooker*
    c. *Ally McBeal*
    d. *Hill Street Blues*

14. While he often appeared on TV as himself, what show did Kenny Rogers guest star on as a diabetic photographer?
    a. *Touched by an Angel*
    b. *The Waltons*
    c. *Highway to Heaven*
    d. *Dr. Quinn Medicine Woman*

15. Which show did Pat Benatar guest star on as the owner of a drug rehab facility (this also marked the only time she appeared on a show as a character, rather than as herself)?
    a. *Dharma and Greg*
    b. *Ally McBeal*
    c. *Family Law*
    d. *The Practice*

16. Which other member of Bruce Springsteen's E Street Band appeared with Steven Van Zandt on *The Sopranos*?
    a. Max Weinberg
    b. Clarence Clemons
    c. Patty Scialfa
    d. None of his bandmates have appeared on the show

17. Which member of Springsteen's band has appeared on *The Wire*?
    a. Max Weinberg
    b. Clarence Clemons
    c. Patty Scialfa
    d. Steven Van Zandt

18. On *Family Matters*, who gave a confidence-building makeover to visiting Aunt Oona, played by Donna Summer?
    a. Harriette
    b. Carl
    c. Laura
    d. Eddie

19. Before Jon Bon Jovi was *Ally McBeal*'s handy man, who did he date on *Sex and the City*?
    a. Carrie
    b. Samantha
    c. Charlotte
    d. Miranda

20. What kind of audition does Fran get, thanks to Sammy (played by Ray Charles) on *The Nanny*?
    a. Back-up studio singer
    b. Chorus member in Broadway play
    c. Editorial commentator on news
    d. Radio announcer

ANSWERS			
1. a	**6.** b	**11.** c	**16.** d
2. b	**7.** b	**12.** a	**17.** b
3. d	**8.** b	**13.** b	**18.** a
4. c	**9.** a	**14.** d	**19.** a
5. c	**10.** b	**15.** c	**20.** c

WAS JERRY SEINFELD ON BENSON?

Yes, he was. In fact, many stars that we think became successes overnight, actually got their starts with smaller roles. Of course, at the time, we had no idea who they were. So, it didn't mean much when Jay Leno appeared as one of Laverne's boyfriends on *Laverne and Shirley*. Or when David Letterman made an appearance on *Mork and Mindy* as an inspirational speaker. Or when Jerry Seinfeld worked for the governor on *Benson*.

How much do you remember about these stars before they were stars?

1. Before he was spinning records as Johnny Fever on *WKRP in Cincinnati*, Howard Hesseman appeared as an attorney on *Soap* and on several prime-time dramas, but his first appearance came on which sitcom?
   a. *The Bob Newhart Show*
   b. *The Andy Griffith Show*
   c. *Rhoda*
   d. *Sanford and Son*

2. Before Jack and Will lived across the hall from each other on
   Will and Grace, what show did they both appear on, although
   not together?
   a. *Baywatch*
   b. *Le Femme Nikita*
   c. *Silk Stalkings*
   d. *The Outer Limits*

3. Before he signed up for *Third Watch*, Coby Bell appeared on
   L.A. Doctors and which other medical series?
   a. *Chicago Hope*
   b. *ER*
   c. *St. Elsewhere*
   d. *Becker*

4. While Penny Marshall worked as Oscar's secretary on *The
   Odd Couple* before she worked at the brewery on *Laverne and
   Shirley*, which sitcom was actually the first she appeared on?
   a. *Chico and the Man*
   b. *The Mary Tyler Moore Show*
   c. *Love American Style*
   d. *That Girl*

5. A year before he became The Fonz on *Happy Days*, Henry
   Winkler showed up at a dinner party on which sitcom?
   a. *The Mary Tyler Moore Show*
   b. *The Bob Newhart Show*
   c. *Maude*
   d. *Here's Lucy*

6. Almost ten years before *Ally McBeal*, Calista Flockhart appeared
   on which daytime soap?
   a. *As the World Turns*
   b. *The Young and the Restless*
   c. *General Hospital*
   d. *Guiding Light*

7. Before landing the comic role of Alex P. Keaton on *Family Ties*, which drama did Michael J. Fox appear on?
   a. *Trapper John, M.D.*
   b. *Family*
   c. *Lou Grant*
   d. All of the above

8. How did *Gilmore Girls'* Lauren Graham make things awkward for Jerry when she appeared as his girlfriend Valerie on *Seinfeld*?
   a. She made him #1 on her speed dial, replacing her stepmother
   b. She looked like two different women, depending on how the light hit her
   c. She had "man-hands"
   d. She preferred to be naked most of the time

9. While Kim Cattrall is best known as Samantha on *Sex and the City*, she's appeared on a wide variety of shows, including *Charlie's Angels*, *Starsky and Hutch*, and as a voice on Rugrats. What drama was her first?
   a. *Trapper John, M.D.*
   b. *Family*
   c. *Quincy*
   d. *Switch*

10. Who did Helen Hunt appear as on *The Mary Tyler Moore Show*, years before her Emmy-winning run as Jamie on *Mad About You*?
   a. Lou's daughter
   b. Murray's daughter
   c. Mary's niece
   d. Ted's niece

11. A year before he was Superman on *Lois and Clark*, what did Dean Cain's character Rick incorrectly believe about Brenda on *Beverly Hills 90210*?
    a. She was French
    b. She was pregnant
    c. She was a teacher
    d. She was a nurse

12. Tony Shaloub appeared on all of the following shows before *Monk*, but which one was he on before he appeared as Antonio on *Wings*?
    a. *The X-Files*
    b. *Frasier*
    c. *The Equalizer*
    d. *Ally McBeal*

13. Which show did George Clooney appear on before he dated Carol Hathaway on *ER*?
    a. *Facts of Life*
    b. *Roseanne*
    c. *Sisters*
    d. All of the above

14. Before he was private eye Spenser or Dan Tana, what show did Robert Urich appear on as a police officer?
    a. *S.W.A.T.*
    b. *Soap*
    c. *Little House on the Prairie*
    d. *Tabitha*

15. On which show did Tom Selleck appear as a private eye before he starred as Thomas Magnum?
    a. *Baretta*
    b. *The Rookies*
    c. *Charlie's Angels*
    d. *The Rockford Files*

16. While he got his start on the *Another World* spin-off *Somerset*, which prime-time series did Ted Danson first appear on?
    a. *Cheers*
    b. *Taxi*
    c. *Laverne and Shirley*
    d. *Amazing Spider-man*

17. Best known for his roles in the dramas *Nash Bridges* and *Miami Vice*, Don Johnson also appeared on which 1970s drama?
    a. *Streets of San Francisco*
    b. *The Rookies*
    c. *Kung Fu*
    d. All of the above

18. Before he was Sonny Crockett's partner on *Miami Vice*, Philip Michael Thomas appeared on several other dramas. Which of these was he on first?
    a. *Medical Center*
    b. *Toma*
    c. *Starsky and Hutch*
    d. *Police Woman*

19. The season before Bruce Willis made his starring debut on *Moonlighting*, which drama did he appear on?
    a. *Miami Vice*
    b. *Simon and Simon*
    c. *Murder She Wrote*
    d. *Remington Steel*

20. While *Desperate Housewives'* star Eva Longoria got her break on *The Young and the Restless*, which prime-time show did she first appear on?
    a. *Law and Order*
    b. *Dharma and Greg*
    c. *Beverly Hills 90210*
    d. *Everybody Loves Raymond*

ANSWERS

1. b	6. d	11. a	16. d
2. c	7. d	12. c	17. d
3. b	8. a	13. d	18. b
4. d	9. c	14. a	19. a
5. a	10. b	15. d	20. c

"COURTESY OF FRED'S TWO FEET"*

Cartoons have often been dismissed as Saturday morning fodder. Recent hits like *The Simpsons* and *King of the Hill* have changed that somewhat, as have the popularity of cable successes like *SpongeBob SquarePants*.

How much do you remember about these cartoons?

1. What was the name of SpongeBob's pet snail?
   a. Patrick
   b. Gary
   c. Monroe
   d. Rover

2. Which was the first cartoon to air during prime time?
   a. *The Simpsons*
   b. *The Flintstones*
   c. *Beavis and Butthead*
   d. *Mighty Mouse Playhouse*

---

*from the theme to *The Flintstones*

3. Who did Racer X turn out to be on *Speed Racer*?
  a. Speed's father, Pops
  b. Speed's uncle, Ray
  c. Speed's brother, Rex
  d. His identity was never revealed

4. What did Fry do for a living before he was accidentally frozen and awakened in the year 2999 on *Futurama*?
  a. Bike messenger
  b. Pizza delivery guy
  c. Convenience store clerk
  d. Bus driver

5. On whose animated short did Woody Woodpecker first appear?
  a. Andy Panda
  b. Mighty Mouse
  c. Donald Duck
  d. Porky Pig

6. In which city was the Pokemon Center located?
  a. Pewter City
  b. Silver City
  c. Gold City
  d. Viridian City

7. Which of Bugs Bunny's programs was the first?
  a. *Bugs Bunny Road Runner Show*
  b. *Bugs Bunny and Tweety Show*
  c. *Bugs Bunny Looney Tunes Comedy Hour*
  d. *Bugs Bunny Show*

8. Who was the first celebrity to appear as himself on *The Simpsons*?
   a. Larry King
   b. Ringo Starr
   c. Tony Bennett
   d. Michael Jackson

9. What does the sign outside the Phillips Broadcasting building claim it used to be on *The Critic*?
   a. Fox
   b. Phillips Radio
   c. Duke Phillips Bait and Tackle
   d. Duke Phillips House of Chicken and Waffles

10. What show did *Pinky and the Brain* originally appear on?
    a. *Tiny Toons*
    b. *Johnny Quest*
    c. *Animaniacs*
    d. *Family Guy*

11. Why did Bobby get hit in the face with a baseball on the first episode of *King of the Hill*?
    a. He was distracted by a hot dog vendor
    b. He was distracted by seeing Connie in the stands
    c. He was distracted by Hank, offering advice from the bleachers
    d. He closed his eyes as the ball was coming at him

12. What was the name of the dog that appeared on the *Tom and Jerry* cartoons?
    a. Rover
    b. Spike
    c. Gary
    d. He was never named

13. Who joined *The Jetsons*'s family on that show's first episode?
   a. Astro
   b. Rosey the Robot
   c. Mac the Robot
   d. Rudy the Computer

14. Who was the first to kill Kenny on *South Park*?
   a. Ned
   b. Alien visitors
   c. Office Barbrady
   d. Mr. Garrison

15. Which regular on *Rowan and Martin's Laugh-In* was the voice of the original *Space Ghost*?
   a. Arte Johnson
   b. Gary Owens
   c. Henry Gibson
   d. Dave Madden

16. What city was under the protection of *Darkwing Duck*?
   a. Metropolis
   b. Duck City
   c. St. Canard
   d. St. Pigeon

17. Who was Dexter's rival on *Dexter's Laboratory*?
   a. Dee Dee
   b. Mandark
   c. Major Glory
   d. Agent Honeydew

18. Which of these shows was the first to feature Scooby-Doo?
    a. *Scooby-Doo Show*
    b. *Scooby-Doo, Where Are You?*
    c. *Scooby's All-Star Laff-a-Lympics*
    d. *Scooby-Doo/Dynomutt Hour*

19. Who was the villain (who hated the *Power Puff Girls*) that was accidently created by the chemicals that were used by Professor Utonium to create the girls?
    a. Him
    b. Mojo Jojo
    c. Fuzzy Lumpkins
    d. Rodwy Ruff Boys

20. Who was the *Teenage Mutant Ninja Turtles*'s Channel 6 reporter friend?
    a. April Carter
    b. April Nolan
    c. April O'Neill
    d. April Jacobs

ANSWERS			
1. b	**6.** d	**11.** c	**16.** c
2. b	**7.** d	**12.** b	**17.** b
3. c	**8.** c	**13.** b	**18.** b
4. b	**9.** d	**14.** c	**19.** b
5. a	**10.** c	**15.** b	**20.** c

THE CURSE OF SAM AND DIANE

The idea of will-they-or-won't-they relationships may not have been new, but it certainly was perfected on *Cheers*. That's the show where we all watched, wondering when, and how, they were finally going to get together. First, he wanted her. Then, she wanted him. Never at the same time. It was innovative, especially for a sitcom. And it became a dance that was repeated ad infinitum. David and Maddie on *Moonlighting*. Harm and Mac on *JAG*. Ross and Rachel on *Friends*.

How much do you remember about these shows about unrequited (or eventually requited) love?

1. Who told Diane about her publishing opportunity on *Cheers*, breaking her and Sam up for the last time (well, before the last episode, that is)?
   a. Frasier Crane
   b. Lilith Crane
   c. Sumner Sloane
   d. Sam Malone

2. Who made a comment about a present Ross left for Rachel, which led her to realize his feelings for her on *Friends*?
   a. Monica
   b. Chandler
   c. Joey
   d. Phoebe

3. Who played Maddie's last love interest before she finally got together with Dave on *Moonlighting*?
   a. Charles Rocket
   b. Mark Harmon
   c. Tom Selleck
   d. Judd Nelson

4. When Mac finally broke things off with Mic Brumby and ran to Harm's apartment on *JAG*, who did she find in his arms?
   a. Diane
   b. Chloe
   c. Renee
   d. Catherine

5. Where did Tony get a job offer from, which nearly split him and Angela up for good on *Who's the Boss*?
   a. University of Iowa
   b. University of Illinois
   c. University of Indiana
   d. University of Ohio

6. Who accidently told Daphne about Niles's feelings for her on *Frasier*?
   a. Martin
   b. Frasier
   c. Donny
   d. Roz

7. Who was Liz dating when she met, was saved by, and fell in love with Max on *Roswell*?
   a. Kyle
   b. Alex
   c. Geoffrey
   d. Milton

8. On *Spin City*, after Charlie and Caitlin finally kiss, who interrupted them before their relationship could go any further?
   a. Paul
   b. Stuart
   c. The Mayor
   d. Mike

9. When Angel asked the Powers That Be to turn him back into a vampire so he can protect Buffy on *Angel*, who said of him, after the sacrifice he had made, he was "not a lower being"?
   a. Cordelia
   b. Spike
   c. Female Oracle
   d. Connor

10. While Mulder and Scully's first kiss was technically with a past-life version of Scully, on what holiday was their real first kiss on *The X-Files*?
    a. Halloween
    b. Thanksgiving
    c. Christmas
    d. New Year's Eve

11. Where did Laura and *Remington Steele* go on their honeymoon?
    a. Mexico
    b. Paris
    c. Egypt
    d. Australia

12. What happened to Amanda on her honeymoon with Lee on the final season of *Scarecrow and Mrs. King*?
   a. She was kidnapped
   b. She got amnesia
   c. She was mistaken for a double agent
   d. She was shot

13. Whose wedding was cancelled at the end of the series run of *Hotel*, once the show itself had been cancelled?
   a. Peter and Christine's
   b. Peter and Devon's
   c. Keith and Julie's
   d. Keith and Christine's

14. Why had Clark decided to leave Metropolis, when he kissed Lois for the first time, on *Lois and Clark: The New Adventures of Superman*?
   a. Metropolis was hit by a heat wave that was being blamed on Superman
   b. Lex Luther had bought *The Daily Planet* and fired him
   c. Metropolis was hit by its first earthquake, which was blamed on Superman
   d. Lois got engaged to Lex Luther

15. Where were Hawkeye and Hot Lips headed when they sought shelter after coming under enemy fire, and wound up in each other's arms for their only romantic get-together on *M*A*S*H*?
   a. Tokyo
   b. Seoul
   c. The 8063rd
   d. I-Corps

16. Once they finally got married, where did Whitley and Dwayne go on their honeymoon on *A Different World*?
    a. Hawaii
    b. Miami
    c. Bermuda
    d. Los Angeles

17. At the end of *The Wonder Years*, when Kevin and Winnie ended up going their separate ways, where did Winnie go?
    a. Hollywood to try acting
    b. New York to try acting
    c. France to study art
    d. Italy to study art

18. Where were Joel and Maggie headed when they finally got together on the last season of *Northern Exposure*?
    a. Anchorage
    b. St. Petersburg
    c. New York
    d. Portland

19. Where did Sydney and Vaughn have their first romantic date on *Alias*?
    a. Germany
    b. France
    c. Italy
    d. England

20. How long did the show *Ed* last after Ed and Carol finally got married?
    a. One season
    b. Six months
    c. Three episodes
    d. They were married on the last episode

ANSWERS

1. c	**6.** b	**11.** a	**16.** d
2. b	**7.** a	**12.** d	**17.** c
3. b	**8.** d	**13.** b	**18.** b
4. c	**9.** c	**14.** a	**19.** b
5. a	**10.** d	**15.** c	**20.** d

GOODBYE, FAREWELL, AND AMEN

Some of the most memorable television episodes are the last ones. The Korean War ended and the members of the 4077th headed home. Everyone, except for Ted Baxter, was fired. The Solomon family headed back to their home planet.

We watched, hoping that Tony would come back to Angela, that Mulder and Scully would find the answers, and that *Seinfeld* would live up to the hype.

How much do you remember about these shows' final episodes?

1. Who was the last one shown testifying against Jerry, Elaine, George, and Kramer on the final episode of *Seinfeld*?
   a. Soup Nazi
   b. Babu
   c. Mr. Pitt
   d. George Steinbrenner

2. Who spoke the last line on the last episode of *Friends*?
   a. Rachel
   b. Monica
   c. Ross
   d. Chandler

3. On the final episode of *The Fugitive*, who revealed that they'd seen the one-armed man kill Kimble's wife?
   a. Leonard Taft
   b. Billy Taft
   c. Lloyd Chandler
   d. Philip Gerard

4. Who guest-starred as the new station owner who ended up firing everyone but Ted on the last episode of *The Mary Tyler Moore Show*?
   a. Johnny Carson
   b. David Ogden Steirs
   c. Vincent Gardenia
   d. Alex Rocco

5. Which employee of Cage and Fish (and McBeal) got married on the last episode of *Ally McBeal*?
   a. John Cage
   b. Richard Fish
   c. Elaine Vassal
   d. Vonda Shepard

6. On the last episode of *Three's Company*, who moved to Hawaii?
   a. Janet
   b. Terri
   c. Jack
   d. Larry

7. How much money did Brian and Joe find in their treasure hunt on the last episode of *Wings*?
   a. $1,000,000
   b. $500,000
   c. $250,000
   d. $150,000

8. Which of the main characters from *The Andy Griffith Show* stayed behind to be part of the cast of *Mayberry RFD*?
   a. Barney Fife
   b. Floyd the barber
   c. Aunt Bee
   d. Thelma Lou

9. Where did Gomer go after he got out of the Marines on the last episode of *Gomer Pyle, USMC*?
   a. Back to Mayberry
   b. To visit his cousins in Beverly Hills
   c. To visit his cousins in Hooterville
   d. Gomer didn't get out of the Marines on the last episode

10. Who was conspicuously absent from the last episode of *Home Improvement*?
    a. Wilson
    b. Al
    c. Heidi
    d. Randy

11. Where did *Frasier* wind up on his show's last episode?
    a. San Francisco
    b. Chicago
    c. Seattle
    d. Boston

12. Who got married on the last episode of *Homicide: Life on the Street*?
    a. Lewis
    b. Bayliss
    c. Munch
    d. Giardello

13. On the last episode of *Barney Miller*, who wound up getting reassigned to a K-9 unit?
    a. Wojo
    b. Harris
    c. Dietrich
    d. Fish

14. Which *M*A*S*H* cast member left and then had to come back on the series's final episode?
    a. Hawkeye
    b. Charles
    c. B. J.
    d. Klinger

15. While Joanie and Chachi's wedding was intended to be the last episode of *Happy Days*, five more episodes aired—on the actual final episode, Leopard Lodge pledges Fonzie, Chachi, and Roger have to follow whose orders?
    a. Howard's
    b. Potsie's
    c. Ralph's
    d. Al's

16. On the final episode of *Night Court*, who turned out to be an alien?
    a. Harry
    b. Dan
    c. Roz
    d. Bull

17. Whose wedding was part of the series' finale of *Magnum, P. I.*?
   a. Rick's
   b. T. C.'s
   c. Higgins's
   d. Magnum's

18. Who was planning to adopt a baby from China on the last episode of *Sex and the City*?
   a. Carrie
   b. Samantha
   c. Miranda
   d. Charlotte

19. Where did Alex land a job on the last episode of *Family Ties*?
   a. New York
   b. Boston
   c. Philadelphia
   d. Washington, D.C.

20. Who did John Walton sell Walton's Mill to on the last episode of *The Waltons*?
   a. Jim Bob
   b. Ben
   c. John Boy
   d. Jason

ANSWERS			
1. b	**6.** b	**11.** b	**16.** d
2. d	**7.** c	**12.** c	**17.** a
3. c	**8.** c	**13.** a	**18.** d
4. c	**9.** d	**14.** c	**19.** a
5. b	**10.** d	**15.** b	**20.** b

ABOUT THE AUTHOR

Ken Kessler is a writer and morning show radio producer in Washington, D.C. He had an early interest in writing, earning an honorable mention in a high school writing competition in Raleigh, North Carolina. This competition was judged by Lee Smith, among others. He went on to study with Lee Smith and science fiction novelist John Kessel at North Carolina State University. He also became a member of the Horror Writers of America (which became the Horror Writers' Association soon after).

While at North Carolina State, he wrote for the college newspaper. His first article was about the state of television, celebrating the debut of *Cheers* and deriding the longevity of *Happy Days*.

Ken also worked at the college radio station, where he was bitten by the radio bug. Radio became his career path, and he spent the next seventeen years "packing and unpacking, traveling from town to town, up and down the dial." He has been part of morning shows in Raleigh, Cincinnati, and Baltimore.

He is currently a producer for Doug Stephan's *Good Day*, a morning radio program heard in more than four hundred markets across the United States on the *Radio America Network*, as well as on the Cable Radio Network and Sirius Satellite Radio.